CROSSROADS IN AFRICA

Crossroads in Africa

Basil Davidson
talks to
Antonio Bronda

Spokesman

First published in Britain in 1980 by Spokesman, Bertrand
Russell House, Gamble Street, Nottingham NG7 4ET

Cloth ISBN 0 85124 245 6
Paper ISBN 0 85124 246 4

Printed by the Russell Press Ltd., Nottingham

Contents

Preface

It is a sorry commentary on the ignorance of the British Labour Movement of African affairs today that a book by one of the most distinguished members of our movement, who has devoted the last 30 years of his life to African studies, should need a preface to introduce him to Spokesman readers. The irony is that much the greater because this interview on Africa at the crossroads was given first to a prominent Italian journalist, who is a specialist in British affairs, for working class readers in Italy who would need no such introduction to Basil Davidson. The interview is especially valuable for British readers because this internationally renowed scholar, who has done so much to put the study of African history in its rightful place, has, for once, and very briefly, in this interview revealed how he came from a deep commitment to the Labour Movement in Britain to devote himself to understanding and supporting the liberation of the African people.

Basil Davidson is one of a long line of distinguished British socialists — one could cite William Morris, H.N. Brailsford, J.A. Hobson, Olive Schreiner, Leonard Barnes, and, in our own generation Thomas Hodgkin — who have done so much to rescue us from the accusation of total complicity with imperialist exploitation in Africa. The briefest references in this interview will alert readers of the present generation of young socialists to the quite remarkable early career of the author — as a British liaison officer parachuted into Tito's partisans and as an officer serving with distinction among the Italian partisans in the Second World War, as a leading writer successively with *The Times, The New Statesman* and the *Daily Mirror,* as secretary of the Union of Democratic Control, before leaving Fleet Street and relying on his own creative resources as a free lance. Ironically, we may recognise now how much the African people and our own understanding of their history and liberation movements owe to his differences with the British Establishment, including the Labour Establishment, in the early 1950s.

I count myself privileged to have been a friend of Basil Davidson's for 35 years; and I can well remember my naive expectation that his commitment to the British Labour Movement and his unrivalled knowledge of Africa would be recognised and utilised by the Labour Party when it was returned to power in 1964 after 12 long years in the wilderness. It was not; and *he* was not surprised. The Tories have always made full use of their own network of expert advisers. The Labour Party in government has never turned with any enthusiasm to the alternative connection of experts that they could have called upon. It has been a disastrous omission. The result is that, whereas throughout Africa, across the black population of the United States and in many countries of Europe — East and West — Basil Davidson's name is a household word among socialists, it is much less well known in Britain. Never was the adage truer that "a prophet is not without honour save in his own country".

The publication of this interview, however, has a greater significance than that of re-establishing Basil Davidson's name in our Movement. It serves to establish also the importance of what he has been doing for 25 years in re-constructing Africa's pre-colonial history and relating it to what is happening in Africa today. It would be tempting perhaps for some to assume from the depth and breadth of erudition of Basil Davidson's books on African history that he had escaped from the day to day struggle for socialism into a comfortable academic retreat. The very opposite is the truth. The history of the African peoples has been sought by this author in order to throw light on what is happening today and to bring African history to bear upon African development where only European history existed before in the minds as much of Africans as of Europeans. A historian who marches hundreds of miles with African guerillas in Guinea Bissau or Angola to share with them their practice and conception of liberation struggle must be a very special type of historian for us; and for the African liberation movements a man who had served with Yugoslav and Italian partisans must have seemed a very special type of European.

It would, however, be quite mistaken to see only the man and his qualities in this interview. What is of far greater importance is what he has to say. The interview was orignally given to an Italian journalist and directed to the Italian Labour Movement. That movement has much in common with our own trade union and Labour Movement and British readers will not feel at all estranged from the questions of an Italian journalist and the answers given. What has to be emphasised is the much greater relevance of these questions and answers to our Labour Movement even than to that in Italy. This is partly because the British Labour Movement was corrupted by Imperialist propaganda for much longer and has greater difficulty, therefore, in seeing Africans as equals, but more important, because British capitalism still has the strongest and most complex connections with Africa. The drive by the present Conservative government to recognise Bishop Muzorewa's rule in Rhodesia, the links of British capital with Kenya and Nigeria, the involvement of British capital above all in South Africa, all indicate a continuing special relationship of British capitalism with Africa.

This interview is not, however, primarily about the remaining ties of foreign capital with African development. It has a wider perspective, embracing the whole enormous task of the African people in throwing off the colonial yoke and establishing their own forms of democratic political development. Almost all the aspects of African neo-colonial development which we most deplore in Uganda or Zaire, in the Central Africa "Empire" or Rhodesia, can be shown to be the direct result of what colonial rule for 70 years created. At the same time it is far from true that the alternative model of the Soviet system is accepted by them as in any way meaningful for African development.

In the interview Basil Davidson comes back again and again to the central problem of African nationalism. What African liberation movements inherited from their colonial masters was a "national" frontier that had no historical meaning before the late nineteenth century European partition of Africa and no linguistic or demographic rationale. The African states which were born of decolonisation agreed in 1964 to accept these divisions, although Ethiopia with its own imperial hold over Eritrea and the Somali Ogaden (in Ethiopia) must be regarded as exceptional. The result is a quite illogical chequerboard of African states which have the only advantage that "national" liberation movements have appealed to a wider interest than those of local and tribal loyalties. The development of European capitalism and its successors in North and South America, in Japan and elsewhere, and even more the development of State planned economies of Russia and Eastern Europe, have been firmly grounded in the nation state. The state was the creation of a national bourgeoisie. The crucial agency of economic development was a developed national middle class. Whether, as in the beginning, development took place through private capital accumulation or, as later in Eastern Europe and elsewhere, through State capital accumulation, a middle class — bourgeoisie or bureaucrat — was the prime mover and the nation-state the essential framework, much more essential than is often allowed for in liberal interpretations of capitalist history.

The central argument of this interview arises from Basil Davidson's conviction that neither capitalist nor centrally planned state development are options that are open to the African liberation movements. A middle class elite could form, and is already forming in Kenya and Nigeria, and this provides the necessary agency linking the state and capital accumulation, often in the most corrupt and corrupting manner. It may help readers if I rehearse here the suggested reasons for Basil Davidson's conviction that this cannot guarantee self-generating and self-reliant economic development.

The first reason is that they are too late. The international links of capitalism are too strong now for any new state to break out of and establish a separate independent development. The escape route from under-development via state protection of industry, which the USA, Germany, Japan and Russia followed, is now closed to all except the most self-sufficient and gigantic populations like the Chinese. For the rest the power of international capital and the scale of technological advance present insuperable obstacles to a process of capital accumulation that is independent of the existing centres of capital and, therefore, free from their centripetal force. It is not only that the technology is owned by the developed countries but that it requires elites like those of the developed countries to operate it and to build it. Even China is finding the way hard without making major con-

cessions to the technology and accumulation of the capitalist
world.

The second reason why capitalist state or state capitalist
economic development is ruled out for the African liberation
movements is that they have depended, and still depend, on mass
participation. This would have to be destroyed if the standard
model of capital accumulation were followed whether by private
capitalists or by the state or by both together. The essence of
such capital accumulation is that, either by force or by fraud,
or a mixture of the two, a proportion of the wealth generated
today has to be extracted from working people to be invested in
development for tomorrow. No industrial revolution has ever
been carried through except by holding down workers' wages or
holding down farmers' prices to a bare subsistence. You cannot
ask people voluntarily to give up the little extra they have above
subsistence to a capitalist, bureaucrat or dictator, from the
countryside to the towns, so that development takes place. If you
want to have mass participation *and* economic development, the
masses will have to participate in all the points of development.
Only the Chinese have tried through developing industry *and*
agriculture in the communes to overcome the exploitation that
industrialisation has meant elsewhere — and they have not wholly
succeeded. Can the Africans do better?

Basil Davidson is optimistic, at least in relation to those
Africans who have liberated themselves through struggle, and this
book reveals step by step with a wealth of personal experience
the grounds for his optimism. These are complex and related to
Africa's long history and to the particular circumstances of the
liberation struggles. They cannot be easily summarised, but
running through Basil Davidson's argument here there is a central
thread of historical consciousness — not the Stalinist distortion of
Marx's historical and dialectical materialism that is widely supposed
to provide a predetermined successful socialist outcome to social
and economic development, let alone the even more vulgar
'historicism' of Rostow's stages of economic growth, but rather
that the African people in rediscovering their past from the
overlay of European interpretations have, in so doing, discovered
their future.

This little book adds much to our understanding of that
process of rediscovery and reveals something of Basil Davidson's

role in it. It is an exciting and encouraging story that we urgently need to understand. Time is running out for all of us on this planet and the corollary of Basil Davidson's optimism is that, if we don't understand each other's histories better — European, African or Asian — and recognise each other's rights — black and white, brown and yellow, but go on fighting each other for privilege and position in Africa and everywhere else, then our fate is sealed. In so many ways Africa, and particularly Southern Africa, is for us in Britain a test case of our capacity for human understanding and common action.

Michael Barratt Brown
September 1979

I

In Search of Africa

Africa is increasingly a barometer of international significance, a pointer on the way to development and emancipation and on the hard testing ground of progress and participation. To quote from your latest book, Africa in Modern History *(1978), "Africans, as a chief branch of mankind, have moved into the modern world and become fully part of it". Yet serious doubts persist on how they are to claim their rightful place in tomorrow's world. At one time great hopes were harboured, but while some promises have been fulfilled, many others have ended in mistakes and tragedies. In some cases early progress towards nationhood and democracy has been overtaken by authoritarian rule and military dictatorship. I would like to unravel, with your help, some of the more significant elements of the complex picture through history to the present, and consider what the position of Africa is today.*

Great hopes were raised, twenty five years ago, and it is perfectly true that some of these hopes have proved to be illusory. That can't be surprising if you consider the African continent from an historical point of view. There are today upwards of 400 million people in Africa. These 400 million are divided into some 43 states and still into several colonies. Nobody can be surprised that there are a very large number of problems which are completely unresolved and many others that are only partially resolved. The important thing for us in Europe, I think, is to look at Africa not simply from the standpoint of day-to-day events, however interesting these may be, but above all from an historical standpoint. It's only when you look at these vast and complex problems from the standpoint of a fairly long sweep of history that you can begin to see where the dominant lines of influence run and are likely to continue to run.

We've seen unfulfilled hopes, deflated expectations, plans that have come to a sad end. It would not be too difficult to paint a dismal picture of the whole continent, but human development never stands still and we have to look for the potential forces that can sustain hope for the future.

Yes, clearly, we have to look at the African situation, *any* African situation, as part of a process: obviously, a dialectical process — subject, that is, to its own contradictions and possible resolutions. The interesting question is: how? And in answering that I'm led back to our own situation of, say, 30 years ago, when I myself first began to try to understand the Africans. In Europe or anywhere else, at that time, there was effectively *no body of knowledge* which could be said to be African history.

Why does Africa, which is geographically so close to us, seem so alien to our culture and understanding?

So far as the recent history of Europe is concerned, this phenomenon of ignorance, of misunderstanding and misinterpretation, was a consequence of the imperialist epoch. Capitalist expansion coincides effectively with the major development of the slave trade after about 1650 and continues through that period until you reach the period of outright intrusion and imperialist invasion in the period of monopoly capitalism, after about 1880. It is true there had been some invasions before that time (the French invaded Algeria in 1830), but broadly speaking the slave trade leads into the colonial period, between 1850 and 1880, and it is in this period that there grew up in Europe not simply a fear of strangers or the old exotic racism which you find for instance in Shakespeare's *Othello*. That was, if you like, a kind of provincial reaction to something strange and exotic. We can't call it racism in the sense that we understand that word today. Racism, in the sense of believing that one race (in this case the so-called white race) is inherently and naturally and inevitably superior to the so-called black race (although very few of them are black as indeed very few of us are white) is a characteristic product of the slave trade and, even more, of the colonial period between about 1880 and 1960. In this whole period it was taken for granted that the Africans were savages. Some exception might be made for the Muslim peoples of North Africa, who were said to be civilised to

the extent that they had become subject to the influence of
Middle Eastern Islam and so on. But the rest of Africa, even to
this day, is said by the same racist mythology to be in some
humanly inherent way different from and inferior to North
Africa, and to consist of people who have no history. We have it
very clearly indeed in our own academic tradition, and right
up to most recent years. I think of a statement by the Regis
Professor of History at Oxford who said textually, in a series of
much publicised lectures given ex cathedra in 1963 (November
20th): "Perhaps in the future there will be some African history
to teach, but at present there is none; there is only the history of
the Europeans in Africa". "So far as the Africans are concerned",
he went on, "there are only the unrewarding gyrations of bar-
barous tribes in picturesque but irrelevant corners of the globe".
This was the standard point of view throughout the colonial
period in Britain and, so far as my reading has gone, in Italy,
in France and elsewhere as well. The history of Africa began,
on this view, round the middle of the nineteenth century with
the penetration of Christian missionaries, followed by explorers,
followed by the colonial enclosure of the continent, so that
all those supposedly savage peoples could be drawn into an
arena of civilisation: naturally, that of Western Europe. You
can see the continuing strength of this particular ethno-centric
"tradition" from that quotation of 1963. For those of us who
rejected this ethno-centrism because we rejected colonialism
(more so because we rejected capitalism), the immediate problem
was obvious. We had to discover pre-colonial African history.
Impossible, said our opponents: you can't discover what isn't
there. But it was there. We deserve no merit just for thinking it
was there, but some, perhaps, for proving the fact. The rise of a
school of historians of Africa, beginning chiefly in this country
and expanding rapidly elsewhere into the USA and France,
really dates from about 1950 when it began to be possible to
put together the findings of archaeologists, linguists, anthropolo-
gists and other disciplines, to recover the old pre-colonial texts,
and to reconsider the old pre-colonial books. With all this, the history of Africa could at least begin to be written. This history is the
basis from which one can now look at the situation as it is today,
and for me it is one of the principal gains of the post war period. It
is not simply that Africa has changed enormously, and enormously

for the better in spite of all the miseries to which you draw attention. It's also that *we* have changed; to a growing extent, we have begun to escape from the fetters of our ethno-centric "tradition". For Europeans this is an absolutely crucial and major advance.

Going back to Victorian times when these myths were created, what do you make of the "organisation of culture" that accompanied the policy of physical intervention, the arrogant assumption that the white man's mode of life was to be the ultimate goal for the African?

I would not think that it was a deliberate policy in the sense that it was a conscious policy. So far as my reading goes it seems much more to have been a logical extension of the kind of ethno-centric chauvinism which had gone together with the whole rise of capitalist Europe. You don't find a conscious attempt to carry out a kind of machiavellian policy which would force the Africans into subjection. What you find is this old ethno-centric assumption that you are dealing with "savages", and so it's your high Victorian duty to "civilise" them. You do this, as Livingstone said, through the blessed process of "Christianity and Commerce". It turns out that "Christianity and Commerce" mean that you dispossess the "savages". You take away their land and use their labour, you banish, kill off or otherwise remove their traders from the scene: you install, in other words, the colonial system or systems (and all the colonial systems were essentially the same in underlying pattern). No matter what fine words might be said, and many were said, the colonial "adventure", this "civilising of the savages", was always and inherently an act of violence: a physical but also a moral violation of an existing and valid order of society. It was physical for all the obvious reasons (the trail of death and disease that "the civilising process" left behind it wherever it went). But it was moral, no less. The physical dispossession went hand in hand with a mental dispossession. There was also the colonisation of minds — of *their* minds but also, we shall do well to remember, of *our* minds as well.

In course of time the imperialist powers, in the period of transnational capitalism, found that they could do without the physical possession of Africa. But still they strove for what we may call mental possession. To be meaningful, therefore, physical de-colonisation has had to go together with mental decolonisation — of *us* as well as of *them*. And it's again in this respect that the proving of the fact of African history (of its real existence in time), and the deepening of our knowledge of that history, have been a valid and even central part of this liberating process we are talking about.

It hasn't been easy, just because its implications are revolution-ary. And it is also true that it has been obliged to meet the danger of being absorbed by those who want to turn history merely into an academic exercise — into another branch, if you like, of academic industry. There has indeed been a very solid effort to reduce the study of African history to a sort of propaganda exercise on behalf of the bourgeois nation-state. That is another aspect of the dialectics of this particular process. We have to see it and react accordingly. In my own judgement, we have to develop ever more consistently a critique of nationalism: we have to resist the concept of nationalism (bourgeois nation-state nationalism in this perspective) as being a permanently "given" *donnée*, eternal, everlasting, a sort of irreplaceable "Platonic form". We have to analyse this nationalism as another part of the same unfolding process. Even so, the net gains are immense. African history is now a many-sided and much-practised discipline, and I regret its weaknesses today far less, infinitely less, than the situation of bland provincial ignorance which it began to displace, some 30 years ago, when we began our work.

In the 50's the history of Africa started to become clearer as the subject aquired intellectual respect. But this was also the time when certain analyses of the social and economic problems of the 'periphery' began to be made and particular theories of under-development in the Third World began to be circulated in univer-sities and political circles. In so far as they raised important issues, those theories certainly performed a useful function, but it progressively became evident that they too were open to serious question. Politically too, events have questioned them again. With the benefit of hindsight, how do you reassess this strand of opinion within the framework of African studies and the more general picture of the Third World?

Here again I think that one needs to recall the situation as it existed in the nineteen fifties. The only way in which the Africans could get out from under the colonial system was to do it on the basis of nationalism. This nationalism had been an idea imported from Europe in the late 19th century where it was presented as the necessary model of any possible development. It was then said to the Africans, for instance in British West Africa, 'when you become a nation, *then* you can become free'. And they naturally used this instrument. They used it sometimes consciously disbelieving in it, but often of course, having had their minds colonised in the same period, they believed that the model of the European nation-state was indeed the right route to a genuine independence in Africa. That was the basis on which the early nationalist parties, or most of them (there were one or two revolutionary exceptions deeply influenced by socialist ideas) accepted the idea of the bourgeois nation-state such as it had developed in Europe since the beginning of the nineteenth century, since the English industrial revolution and the French political revolution. Now this of course, to begin with, seemed very shocking to the controlling classes in Western Europe. They opposed very strongly any idea that Africa could or should become independent except at some very remote time in the distant future, maybe in a hundred years or so. At the same time, in those same 1950s, capitalism itself was undergoing a process of its own development. So far as colonial Africa was concerned, that was partly the fruit of the war. America came out of the war immensely strong, Britain comparatively weak, France very weak indeed. The Americans, moral reasons apart (they may have existed but I am making no judgement on that here), were understandably interested in ending the empires of other people – above all the old-style monopoly-capitalist empires of the "closed doors". A century earlier Britain had insisted on the "open doors" of "free trade" because the British were then incomparably strong; now it was the Americans. They were not in the least interested in territorial possession and enclosure; they were interested in something rather different – an economic enclosure dominated by their own economic interests. So we enter the period of multinational or, as I prefer to call it, trans-national capitalism – the trans-national capitalism of great corporations which remain based, nonetheless, at first in the

US and then, as we know, elsewhere.

Now it was a natural counterpart of this whole process, set in motion by the Americans and soon relayed by the British, that the Africans should become politically free within the structures of an *acceptable* economic system. The Africans could do whatever they liked, according to the doctrine, provided always that what they liked was acceptable to the dominant economic interests of the Western system (later on, you may argue, the dominant Eastern system may adopt its own version of the same approach, but that is not the issue here).

This meant, for a colonial Africa striving to be free, acceptance of the model of the bourgeois nation-state, the capitalist nation-state, as an *instrument* of politics and a *mode* of organisation. And so it was that the structure and implications of this model, in its transferred embodiment to Africa, became installed and enthroned in the 1950s and early 1960s. Being king, this model at once treated all opposition as subversive, or simply as silly, utopian, idealistic — and above all *wrong*. Great efforts were deployed by a positive army of "experts" to insist on this. The "classic text" — that of the American Professor Walt Rostow's *Stages of Economic Growth,* published in 1960 — went through sixteen editions during the 1960s and served as the "Bible of Development". Its essential argument was that all peoples, all states, no matter what their history, go through the same five stages of economic growth, and end, must end, cannot *not* end, in the same blessed destiny: that of the socio-economic condition of the United States of America in its "period of high mass consumption" *circa* 1960. Now for those of us who knew any African history (and by this time many of us did), Rostow's essential theme was no more than an a-historical fantasy. But aside from this, even by 1965 it clearly didn't explain the facts.

It was an over-optimistic linear theory which you didn't take at face value?

Not over-optimistic, simply wrong. My friend Eric Hobsbawm was among the first to point out that what Rostow called "the take off" (the preliminary, that is, to soaring into the blessed skies of "high mass consumption"), was simply another word for "industrial revolution"; and that it was pure fantasy to imagine, and perfectly unserious to suggest, that all nations, all states, approached that process of development through the "same history of stages". Aside from that theoretical critique, what was actually *happening* in Africa during the 1960s was manifestly quite different from what, according to Rostow, *ought* to be happening. What ought to have been happening, according to Rostow, was a process of capital accumulation, deriving from higher levels of productivity and income right across the society in question, and moving steadily towards indigenous industrial investment, and so on. What actually *was* happening, on the contrary, was falling living standards, stagnation in all aspects of productivity (or in most), a widening gap between many poor and few rich, practically no indigenous investment in industrialisation and, along with all that, an institutional collapse of all those *political* structures which, according to Rostow, would protect and enlarge the culture of an emergent bourgeois nation-state.

Faced with all that, those who worked in a generally Marxist tradition of analysis were challenged, even more strongly than before, to develop and elaborate an alternative analysis, if you like an alternative model of possible development. And so it was from about the middle of the 1960s that you began to get the onset of an "alternative scholarship", an "alternative explanation", Marxist in analysis, which started from the groundwork of social structure, class structure, and, together with that, of post-colonial economic relationships. Particular merit has to be given to a number of French thinkers in this respect, Suret-Canale, Coquéry-Vidrovitch, Meillassoux and others who, while often greatly disagreeing among themselves (and perhaps *because* they greatly disagreed among themselves), were able to clear a lot of new ground. On this new ground, we should also note, new African radicals have also taken their stand: while, at the same time, outstanding African revolutionary thinkers such as Amilcar Cabral were also, from about 1964, beginning to produce their own original analyses of the realities they knew.

How did people like you who felt dissatisfied with the existing knowledge, models and theories, go about trying to change the climate of African studies and foster a more realistic appreciation of the problems undistorted by abstract ideologies? superimposed.

Firstly, those who questioned the orthodox analysis, whether we speak of the 1950s or later, were brought up at once against the fact of their own ignorance. Consequently there set in, around that time, a very determined effort to study the reality on the ground. This is another aspect of that intellectual change which I have spoken of earlier. The study of the reality of Africa has gone on in a very intensive and multi-sided way so that the generation of today (those for instance who are 25 to 30 years old) who study Africa, have access to more information than any previous generation in history. This perhaps is the greatest change to have occurred in the European intellectual approach to Africa. It is much greater than in relation to Asia where studies had gone on long before, and much greater than in relation to Latin America. The serious study of Africa is now in a very advanced condition and is carried forward by a community of scholars that is multinational, cross-national, and includes more and more Africans themselves.

You have visited Africa many times, shared in the thoughts and practical experiences of many of the leaders and directly witnessed radical changes in their different countries, revolutions in the making, if you like. How did you first start getting involved in African studies?

That would make a long story about myself and I dislike such "autobiographies". Let me just say that I belong to that generation of children born in the First World War whose destiny it was to fight in the Second World War. I came out of World War II in that wing of the British Labour movement which was deeply convinced that any progress for Britain must depend partly on striking off the chains, to use a cliché, of imperial possession. I thought, with others, that to get rid of the colonies was for us a sovereign benefit, because without getting rid of our colonies we could not fully liberate the potential of our own people, of our own culture. Obviously one also took it for granted that national freedom was a good thing and we hadn't fought through the war in order to accept that Europeans could be free but Africans could not be free. Clearly for the Africans, one took it for granted, freedom must be a sovereign benefit as well. So that was my general approach. But how did I get involved? Well, you know,

one would like to say that one's life had been a long series of
nicely planned steps, one after the other, all of them foreseen;
perhaps some people have been able to plan their lives in that
way, but I alas have not. My original plan, back in 1946 when
with millions of others I had to readjust to the problems of
peace (to personal problems, if you like) was to build on a quite
extensive knowledge of Eastern Europe and become some kind of
"expert" on that area. Blessed innocence: I counted without the
"Cold War". By 1949, in what we may call the "period of mature
Stalinism", it was obvious that visas were going to be very hard to
get, perhaps impossible, and historical research unlikely to be
blessed with any kind of encouragement. All that doesn't matter
any longer, but the personal reason for the difficulty has perhaps
a little interest as a footnote. In 1943-44 I had served with
Yugoslav partisans in the Vojvodina, including the then Hungarian-
occupied zone of the Vojvodina, in the plains north of the
Danube. In 1949 the Stalinists put on trial the then secretary-
general of the Hungarian Communist Party, Rajk László, and
found him guilty of being Tito's "agent". As they had already
"proved" that Tito himself was an "agent of the imperialists",
they had to find a little evidence which fitted into this absurd
"theory of guilt". Of course they couldn't find any evidence,
because none existed. So they found some that did not exist.
They "discovered" that I, as a British officer in Hungarian-
occupied Yugoslavia, had served as the "link" between Rajik and
Tito. You can't really imagine anything sillier, but it "cooked my
goose" for getting visas for Eastern Europe.

So I had to think again about my little plan for a post-war life.
At the time I was writing for *The New Statesman.* And I began
to ask myself, in 1949-50, what my own personal "alternative
model" could be. I found this a difficult thing. Then, one day,
a letter came to me from the leader of a trade union in South
Africa. This was Solly Sachs, a fine and courageous man who
had organised a non-racist (multi-ethnic, that is) Garment Workers'
Union and faced, of course, the inevitable persecutions by the
racist South African state and its various governments. Sachs
died recently in exile in London, but he is a man worthy to be
remembered. He is interesting, too, for another reason. He
belonged to that small Jewish community, in South Africa,
which had arrived there, mostly from one or other part of the

Tsarist Empire, early in this century or at the end of the last. Some of them went into business, became financial crooks and speculators, and made fortunes out of diamonds and gold. Others turned altogether against the system, and became radicals and revolutionaries. Characteristically, all these Jews stood right outside the closed ideological communities of the South African English and Dutch; and they saw the situation with a corresponding objectivity. If they didn't "move in" on the system and make financial careers by "working it", they moved against the system and tried to overturn it. And it's a fact that the whole revolutionary tradition in South Africa has been deeply and creatively influenced by those of them who became radicals and revolutionaries. Sachs was among the radicals and revolutionaries. That's why the trade union he organised was non-racist and anti-racist — Africans as well as Europeans had their place in it. (That was back in those days; today there's no longer any space for such a union in the *apartheid* state). Solly wrote to me, and said: "Look, we've been reading your articles about Europe. Come out here and write about us". I didn't really want to go, I wasn't interested, but it seemed perhaps a useful thing to do.

Of course when I got there and began to move around in South Africa and meet Africans like Kotane, Mandela, Tambo and others, and began to *understand,* I was "captured". I saw that Africa was a vast field for inquiry, and that I was lucky to have "strayed" into it at that particular moment in time. I went back in 1952 to West Africa, in 1953 again to southern Africa (being then deported from South Africa for a book I'd published the year before), to the Belgian Congo and Angola in 1954, and so on. Africa became my own "alternative model". And from desperate ignorance I have at least moved into a position of "knowing what I do not know"; and perhaps that's the beginning of wisdom? Anyway, for me, Solly's letter was a fortunate turn.

Africa is a great and varied continent whose roots go back thousands of years, with an attractive newly born political conscience, a vast place well trodden by white man's boots, be it explorers', soldiers', missionaries', or scholars', a human arena once more to be discovered by those who want to understand it historically on its own terms and properly place it in a rapidly changing modern world. One could make that trip for a variety of reasons and motivations. You went there as a seeker after truth. But there are indirect ways of romanticising even unconsciously one's own impulses – the interest in the old history and culture of "Black Mother Africa" as much as the sympathy for the contemporary national liberation movements. On the other hand one could carry unconsciously remnants of a 'masters' mind' – a spirit of adventure or its opposite, a sense of guilt for the collective exploitation by the West. Hidden trends and feelings that at one time or another might stir in an individual's conscience. If you forgive my asking, what was your attitude when you first went to Africa?

Well, I certainly never felt any sense of personal guilt. How could I have? With countless others, I had gone through the great unemployment and the misery of the 1930s in England. I had learned to understand, and with others I had learned it the hard way, that the exploitation of the Africans had gone hand in hand with the exploitation of my own people. Even if I couldn't have put it so clearly then, one can't confuse a people with a system. One has to ask the old question, "who whom" – and in our case, the English case, it was obvious what the answer was. My starting point, that being so, was that decolonisation might be going to be a good thing for the Africans: but first and foremost, it was going to be a good thing for us. "Romance", yes, possibly: because Africa is immensely thrilling, immensely interesting, intriguing and subtle and very dramatic. Perhaps I have always felt that certain element of romance and I never cease to be excited when I go there. But I think that the motivation of those of us English radicals who went to Africa after the war was very much as I have described. We went to find the means of making a structural change, to decolonise for our sake as well as for theirs. That may sound a bit highminded but if you ask me did I feel a sense of guilt, no, because I saw the whole imperial enterprise as a damage done to us as well as to them.

In your last book you also said that "a history that is close to a writer's heart will always be a history, in a vital because conceptual sense, which is to some extent autobiographical".

What do you feel you have learnt from Africa? Are you a different person now because of this long and deeply-felt involvement in its history?

Well, I hope I am. You remember Brecht's famous story — one of his *Geschichten von Herrn Keuner* — when Mr Keuner meets an old friend and this old friend wanting to be nice to him says 'I haven't seen you for years. You haven't changed at all' and Mr Keuner goes white with shame. This would be my point of view. I would not like to speak much about myself but about that collective group in the broad Labour movement in Britain which has followed this particular line of development. I think that we have changed and, because we have, enormously widened our understanding. It's been a very instructive experience to force oneself through all the inherited prejudices, the inherited myths that we naturally had in our heads, no matter what our point of view was. You go from an imperialist country to Africa and you have to take yourself through a whole "course" of obstacles. You arrive with any amount of prejudices, misunderstandings, mythologies, anxieties, worries and you have to take yourself through all that. I don't say that I've done it successfully, that we did it successfully, but we certainly did try to take ourselves through this obstacle race and we came out at the other end, I think, at least in a very realistic frame of mind. I don't think that we suffered at all from sentimental illusionism.

So, from *this* standpoint, it doesn't bother me at all that Africa today is full of troubles. It doesn't cause me to think that decolonisation has been a "failure". Least of all does it make me think that this decolonisation was "premature": that everything would have been better if decolonisation hadn't begun in the 1950s but decades later, fifty years later, and so on. We thought, and consciously as I recall, that the sooner the better: if only because Africans could not even *begin* to face their real problems of unity and progress until they became free to confront these problems. And they could not become free to do this until they were free of the cultural — and therefore political — chains of the colonial period.

You went to Africa as a researcher and your interest was enlarged by your findings and your scientific analysis of them. But you

*also went there with a political commitment, or at least a feeling
for other peoples' politics. How did these two elements of interest
and commitment combine together in motivating you in your
task of understanding Africa better?*

I think it is the hen and the egg, isn't it, this question of commitment and scholarly objectivity. I don't believe myself that any
historiography is uncommitted. I have never read an uncommitted
historian. Of course there are those who claim to be uncommitted,
but the claim is often a very hollow one. I much admire and
respect the historian who says, "This is my point of view, this
is my commitment, you may balance that off with what I say".
One should distinguish facts from the selection of facts. The
first are objective, the second can never be. All the same, I
think there is such a think as "subjective objectivity": it's that
approach to selection which moves with, unfolds, helps to define
the "movement of history". Historicism? Call it that if you like.
But look at what happens: for example, in this case.

    Back in the early 1950s there were quite a lot of British
historians (and even more French historians) who were writing
about history in Africa. Now at that time Africa was manifestly
moving towards some great change – towards, in short, the end
of the old colonial systems. But what facts did these historians
select? They selected, as before, the facts of European history in
Africa. They told, once again, the story of Livingstone, Stanley,
King Leopold, Cecil Rhodes, all that crowd. Objective facts,
no doubt: but what about the principle of selection? In *fact,* at
that time, the underlying trend of scholarly research in Africa
had entered a new period. Notably in archaeology, to some
extent in social anthropology, even to a smaller extent in the
reassessment of known historical documentation. And *this* was
the trend that was "subjectively objective" – *not* the work of
the orthodox historians repeating in new forms what had long
been said before.

    Again, an example. In 1957 I wished to visit the East African
coast (of Kenya and Tanzania) in order to look at the ruined
sites of the Swahili culture of the 15th century and before.
But the colonial authorities refused to let me in. A piece of
luck, as it proved. I fell back on an alternative. This was to
visit the great ruined site of Meroë 100 miles north of Khartum
in the Sudan (which had become independent a year earlier, so

the colonial authorities couldn't prevent my going, and the Sudanese authorities welcomed me). And I was able to be at Meroë while archaeologists were reaching important new conclusions on its importance in the history of the ancient African empire of Kush — as we know now, a very influential part of ancient African history: in fact, one of the "starting points" for an understanding of subsequent African history, and even, however indirectly, of modern African history. So I began, with others, to fit these "unselected facts", in this case about Meroë, into a history of Africa which was quite different — being centred on the history of the Africans in Africa and not of the Europeans in Africa — from the history of the orthodox historians. But who was more "objective": those who "discovered" the "unselected facts" of African history in a time of decolonisation? Or those who went on selecting new bits of knowledge around what was *already* known about the colonising Europeans?

Another kind of "European paternalism"? I do not think so. As a matter of record, the first historian to produce this kind of history was Onwuka Dike, a Nigerian, and he was by no means alone in trying to do so. All we did, we non-Africans, was to add our effort to an African inspiration, an African intuition, that was already embodied in the culture of the decolonising years. We moved, in short, with "the movement of history". The "interest" and the "commitment" were inseparable, continually reproducing each other: and they led to the enlargement of that "subjective objectivity" which can alone give truth — any aspect of universal truth — to the whole enterprise of historiography.

One might rightfully say that a people deprived of its own history, or prevented from presenting a coherent picture of it to the world, will always be slaves to others who can command the heights of mankind's history. To assist in the reconstruction of African history, or the roots of African civilisation, to help rebuild a sense of identity and dignity, must be an important task, but how exactly do you see your own job?

I am among those who think that history, the study and the explication of human society, has a universalist value, belongs to us all, rises far above the conjunctures of any particular moment or constellation of circumstances. As for how I see my own job —

well, it's to assist in some measure, no doubt a small one, in the
promotion of that "subjective objectivity" that I've been talking
about. And I must say that no serious African scholar has ever
yet accused me – accused us, in our community of radical
scholars – or trying to impose another "outside variant of culture".

But surely there must be more to it: this is no ordinary story, it's
not the history of peoples who are already 'in history' on their
own terms, who have been able to tell others their story in an
autonomous and independent way.

I think that it is a mistake, quite often made in Europe, to
suppose that Africans have in some way remained unconscious
of their own history. But given their historical situation today,
notably in terms of non-literacy, an external scholarship can
certainly help to broaden their consciousness of *what is possible.*
But you asked me how I saw my own job, and I would like to say
a little more about that. My starting point was that the elucidation
of Africa's history could be useful to Africans, but that, in any
case, it *must* be useful to Europeans. How otherwise, in the
period of decolonisation, in this phase of the world as we know
it now, are we Europeans to get ourselves beyond our own
continental provincialism, our racism, our sense of some kind
of "natural and inherent superiority"? The 21st century isn't far
away now, and yet in Britain, at least, it's still pretty much a
question of dragging our dominant culture into the 20th century.
We limp too often on a hollow leg, a leg gone rotten with the
survivals of a 19th century imperialism which cannot be healthy
in the world we live in now.

If we examine the unspoken assumptions of this "hollow leg"
in relation, for example, to African culture, what do we find?
We find, almost invariably (however little admitted nowadays,
outside the parish-pump stupidities of the extreme right), the
declarations of Hegel in his Jena lectures of the 1830s. Yes, the
1830s – when Hegel said that the Africans, having no history,
could not be considered as historical peoples, as peoples worth
considering with the same respect as other peoples. These were
the assumptions that were invariably called in play whenever the
imperialist powers, in a mood of after-dinner moralising, wished
to justify their conquest and dispossession of the Africans. Hegel
had never heard of Meroë and the 800 year-old empire of Kush,

nor of ancient Ghana, nor of Mali, nor of all the other states, large and small, that we now know formed a central part of African history at a time when Germany itself had no historical identity or was divided into little warring states and princedoms. All the same, Hegel felt no qualms about saying that Africans had no history. To destroy that misunderstanding and all the edifice of "moral justification" that was built on it (which still, very often, lives in European minds today) you must show it for what it was. You must compare it with the *facts*. You must portray this "movement of history" over millenia. That we have been able at least *to begin to do this* is, for me, one of the central gains, moral and intellectual, of the second half of the 20th century.

You have said that the new history of Africa flows organically out of the old history of Africa. Are you attempting in your study of the distant and more recent past to get an inkling of the future?

I have been considerably criticised here because people say that the Africans, even if they have a long history of their own, nevertheless in entering the modern world have to accept so many structures and ideas from it that effectively they have to begin again. If they have to begin again then clearly the new history of Africa doesn't flow organically out of the old. This I contest. If you stand as firmly as you can, as firmly as a European person can, on the ground of African history, then you will see that the process of decolonisation is a dual one. It's a question of getting rid of external control (of colonial rule, etc.). It's a question eventually of getting rid not only of political and economic controls, but also cultural control and, if you like, of re-Africanising one's thought. So that's one process. The second process clearly is a dialectical one in which the Africans themselves move consciously out of their own heritage. The revolutions in Africa today, in so far as they are genuine, are revolutions against colonial rule in all its implications. But they are also revolutions against those aspects of the African heritage which are no longer valid in modern terms. It is a question of modernising *what exists,* of rejecting the impositions of the colonial model (or of the "neo-colonial" model, the model of the bourgeois nation-state), while at the same time rejecting all those aspects of African culture and structure which stand in the way of unity and progress. No kind of foreign model can serve instead. What has to be done — what *is being done* in Africa's revolutionary states today — is to import all those technologies from world revolutionary experience which may be useful, but to reshape and re-apply these to an entirely different reality from the reality in which that experience was produced. Only in the measure of its originality — its appropriateness to the actual circumstances of this or that African community today — will the result be viable, successful, capable of development. Beyond all the "demagogy of revolution" (and Africa has suffered a positive diarrheoa of pseudo-revolutionary verbalism), *this* is the substance that encapsulates the African revolution. It is a revolution that will not be, cannot be, a "moment" or a "turning-point", but a long and difficult and continuously fruitful process. We have seen its beginnings. Our children will see its maturity. This is what "the movement of history" means in Africa today.

Some people would like the Africans to accept a new view of history, to aquire a new conception and dimension compatible with our world as it is now. But that would mean substantially perpetuating a static condition of the latter and conforming to accepted standards with their inherent control and discipline.

Alex Haley's Roots, *that much publicised best seller from the USA which has had such wide resonance in the past few years, is the story of Negroes who originated from Africa and in time became assimilated into American society, the industrial world and urban environment. This process of standardisation is perhaps what some people would like to see as a civilising exercise. 'Roots' are no longer what you take with you from your past — culture, memory, instincts and expertise — in the task of equipping yourself for the future, but what you are forced to forget and lose in becoming an integrated member of a highly technological and disciplined society. What do you think of an assimilation that tries to flatten out all differences, to do away with all points of resistance?*

I haven't read *Roots,* but I can see that it is a very useful book in the US today because it talks about the historical origins of the black people of that country, and recalls the facts of enslavement which, I'm bound to say, one might think that Americans had not forgotten. All that is very good and useful. Beyond that, the application of the idea of "roots", as it has often been used in Europe *vis à vis* the black peoples, is a mystification. In any of its variants — Senghor's *Négritude,* or, as others have put it, "la rentrée aux sources" — the search for authentic origins — refers to more or less alienated intellectuals of the colonial and "neo-colonial" period. They have absorbed the culture of the West and accepted its "superiority". At the same time, this culture of the West has rejected them as *persons,* as black persons, and so they react against it. They look for a "synthesis". It is an elegant intellectual occupation, perhaps, but with absolutely no application to the vast majority of Africans. That vast majority are in no sense looking for roots. They are standing on their roots, they are growing out of their roots and suffer no anxiety about that. Their problem is not to find their roots. Their problem is to nourish and develop them in such a way that these roots may produce a new harvest, new flowers, new sources of cultural nourishment in line with the real and pressing needs of today.

This is why "the revolution in Africa", as it develops now and in the years ahead, will be indigenous in form and, at any rate to some extent, in content as well. The "neo-colonial" élites may persist in sowing the ideas of their alienation in independent soil, and hoping that new flowers will grow. The people, the masses, the majority, the revolutionary movements and parties, cannot possibly do that. Unless they are to be false to their own convictions and interests, the masses *have* to act within the framework of indigenous culture. *That* is the culture to which they have to apply, as skillfully as they can, the ideas and organisational forms and the innovations of revolutionary technique. There is no guarantee of the result; but there is also no alternative — except another, if different, phase of external control. This is why, in the measure of their success, the revolutionaries of Africa, whether today or tomorrow, must act in forms and modes that are specific, and are therefore original. It may be banal to repeat it, but no models imposed from the outside, whether by capitalism or socialism, are going to be effective in the Africa that now lies before us. Let me put it another way: in the sense that there is such a thing as "euro-communism" today, there is just as surely in Africa, and in the same sense, an "afro-communism".

II

Confronting History

You have said that the whole process of dismantling the old imperialist structures was beneficial to Africa. After a couple of decades or more, though, old problems have remained unresolved, new ones have arisen that may be even more intractable and there have been quite a few outright disasters. Have these factors led you to revise your opinion at all?

Anyone who has lived through the history of Europe in the last forty to fifty years will not be easily disappointed by the failures of people elsewhere. The answer is no, I don't revise my judgement in any basic or essential way, nor do I think that those of my fellow workers and comrades who have followed the same evolution have done so either or would be inclined to do so. This is for a number of reasons. The first reason is that very considerable gains flowed from the first de-colonisation, from what Amilcar Cabral used to call the struggle against classical colonialism, the gaining of a purely political independence in the late '50s and early '60s. Secondly, because we may observe a considerable development of political thought and action since that "first de-colonisation". The picture of intellectual stagnation that is often presented in our press is in my opinion completely astray. I don't find any such intellectual stagnation. Thirdly one may note, as a fact of some importance, that according to the latest available statistics of the UN, something like 45% of the population of the continent as a whole is under the age of sixteen. It will be manifestly this youthful generation who in the next twenty years will carry this development of new themes, objectives, and ideas much further. That's not to guarantee progress, I don't think that one falls into the trap of supposing that any progress is ever guaranteed. Disaster is possible as well as progress. I'm only pointing to those signs which enable me to say that the relative optimism of thirty years ago remains a relative optimism.

Let me talk a little bit about the gains of the first de-colonising processes which began in the early 1950s with the internal autonomies of a number of British colonies leading on to the eventual political de-colonisation, the political withdrawal of the colonial powers, in the 1960s, and of course, in the case of the Portuguese, as recently as 1975. It has been a long process of de-colonisation, stretching over something like twenty five years and it hasn't been easy. It has been a period of intense self-development for certainly a very large fraction of the population of the whole continent. De-colonisation, when it came, and first of all in West Africa, brought with it very substantial gains, cultural gains more than any other. It brought with it the possibility of throwing off the incubus, the weight of European racism, the belief that Africans were inherently incapable of behaving, achieving and doing the same things, taking the same initiatives as the Europeans. This was a liberating process of very profound value. Look at the novels and poetry, the plays, the music: everything begins to blossom. Round about 1955-65 there is a harvest of new self expression, some of it not good, some of it moderate, some of it very good, just as you'd expect. Yet *all* this was an enormous gain. The second major gain was that Africans could at last begin to find out about the world. They were no longer enclosed within their colonial frontiers. They could travel in the rest of Africa. They could move around. They could become part of the world which the colonial period had prevented them from becoming. You have in the first de-colonisation the necessary beginning of any liberating process in relation to the colonial heritage or in relation to the pre-colonial heritage that we were talking about earlier on. The first big step. And this I think was a step forward which has not been cancelled out. There were substantial gains for us; our own society has become less enchained, less rooted to the past, it has become freer, more concerned with human values than it was in the past. But leaving that aside, let's consider only the African question. There were very considerable gains from the first decolonisation, but the price paid for those gains was also considerable. It consisted in acceptance of the structural implications of decolonisation on the model of the bourgeois nation-state. And we see very well what all that has meant. The cliché phrase for that is neo-colonialism, a phrase much used by Africans over the last ten to fifteen years, meaning of course that the colonial powers retained their effective economic control and often their cultural control while abandoning a political control which they no longer needed. The neo-colonial situation for Africans is manifestly another form of cultural subjection. If you want to see the extraordinary lengths to which it can go, you've only to consider the case of the Emperor Bokassa of the Central African Empire. The Central African Empire is a country containing less than two million people. It is really very poor indeed, one of the countries most impoverished by the whole colonial period. Bokassa, who became the military dictator of it, then, not very long ago, proclaimed himself as emperor, and had himself crowned on the model of the Emperor Napoleon. One can only recall the well known remark of Marx that history repeats itself but only as farce. This was a farce but also a tragedy. It's a tragedy for the people of the Central African Republic who were thrown back into a repressive and ineffective model of some grotesque shadow of the Napoleonic system. That might suit some people in Europe very well indeed. It certainly could suit nobody in the Central African Republic except the Emperor Bokassa and his family clients. That's an extreme case, but if you go right down through the list you will see that the basic problem of Africa since the first decolonisation is the problem of institutional inadequacy. The institutions taken over at the time of the political decolonisation have not worked and manifestly now cannot work. So that now we get into the period when the gains have been accepted and they continue, but the losses become ever greater; and out of this contradiction between gains and losses there must necessarily come a new resolution.

In a negative sense, of course, the turning away from the parliamentary model of the bourgeois nation-state — the constitutional model of the independences of the 1950s and early 1960s — has already gone very far. Many parliaments have entirely disappeared. Others remain, but as little more than decoration; elections continue to be held, but nobody believes they will do any good — save to those who are elected. Portentous economic plans continue to be made: more and more, they are little more than "words in the wind" as the processes of wealth transfer from Africa to the "developed world" not only continue, but even increase in volume and in painfulness. "Aid" is given by the "developed" countries, but has to be paid for by an indebtedness which has now become chronic. Every year, a larger volume of Africa's realisable annual surplus has to be earmarked for paying the debts which have followed "aid". And yet, at the same time, there is also a positive sense in which Africans are beginning to turn away from the "inherited model", and are beginning to shape the foundations of a viable alternative of their own.

From what you say it appears that you retain your basic relative optimism about the development of Africa in spite of its tremendous political and economic problems, the pressures from outside, and its mistakes and failures. Going a bit deeper into past experiences to see what they teach us about this struggle for survival, if you like, about organisation at the institutional level and on the more general political plane, how can Africa put the lessons of history together with a wider knowledge of the modern world? Is there a new model which might be developed from a combination of different factors by Africa itself?

It's a very big question and will go beyond such wisdom as I have got. We don't know if Africa is going to "survive", it may not, it would be sentimental to suggest that it must.

If Africa doesn't find valid alternative models of its own then the present trends will continue. These can be summarised in a very brief and quite unsentimental way. One is that the population is growing at a rate of between 2½% and 3% per year, which means that the 400 million Africans of today become by the year 2000, unless there are unimaginable disasters, 7-800 million, practically double today's number. At the same time the rate of production of food and the necessities of life, if you like the average daily standard of living in so far as that is a real statistic, is not rising but is falling. Available production for consumption is not keeping in step with the increase of population: consequently, there is a trend of impoverishment. A continuing impoverishment is of course perfectly conceivable, and all the other factors we've been talking about add to it. Not only does the system of production not allow consumption to keep up with the rising population but the indebtedness to foreign lenders which I have just mentioned eats into the available surpluses. This mis-spending of government élites, the waste of money, individual corruption — all these things add to the rate of impoverishment; and, if present trends do continue, then of course the future for Africa looks very much as though it will be somewhat like the future of India, at least up to recent years ago. That is to say that there is a vast and terrible problem of what is called overpopulation. I say what is called overpopulation because Africa is relatively underpopulated. Relatively, that is, to a creative and expanding system of production and of relations of production. A system capable of realising the material and human wealth of Africa will undoubtedly need, and be able to sustain at a rising level of everyday life, a population far larger than 400 millions. An eventual total of 800 millions would be nothing to worry about. But as things are *today,* Africa suffers from every symptom of overpopulation. Within *this* system of production and relations of production — internally or in relation to the outside world — the trend is towards catastrophe. India, South America? I don't know. But with whatever differences, it seems to me that the situations are the same: a vast increase of population within systems of production perfectly incapable of supporting people in the future, even at the low level from which they suffer today. A recipe, in short, for endemic famine.

So, if this very dark picture you are drawing should unfortunately come true, the consequences for Africans will be even greater than the serious damage done in the past by all the factors we have discussed.

We can say this: that the prolongation of existing socio-economic structures and world relationships, deriving as these do from the colonial period and the world capitalist structure, must inevitably, without a change, produce in Africa a vast international slum.

And that presumably will have dangerous repercussions at the level of international politics as well, the balance between different systems, coexistence, diplomatic problems and so forth.

It might or it might not, I don't know. I feel it is sufficiently clear that Africa cannot afford to continue on present lines.

I'm speaking not only for myself but I'm trying to translate to you what I believe to be some of the dominant ideas that you will find among progressive Africans today. Of course for most governing groups, often called the ruling elites, the situation may be well enough. In the Belgian Congo, now Zaire, Mr Mobutu can if he wishes continue to export capital to Switzerland and build villas and all the rest of it. For him and his like the situation, no doubt, is rather comfortable. But for the majority of the population, the prospect is, as things are going now, far from happy. In many countries, the outlook for the majority of the people, with the population increasing at the rate of 2½% to 3% a year, is more likely to be extremely bleak. You may ask how is it possible in this situation to maintain an attitude of relative optimism. And I suppose the answer to that is subjective in the sense that people like myself believe that humanity does in historical fact and experience produce its own antidotes, saves itself. This if you like is the product of the life that my generation has had to live. If you could imagine that Hitler and Mussolini had succeeded in 1943, 44, 45, then the outlook for most of us would have been extremely bleak. They didn't succeed because the peoples of Europe were capable of saving themselves. That may sound like a very large and general statement, but I have the same point of view about Africa, and I would defend it by pointing to the dominant trends which are now visible. One finds, in almost every African country, groups of persons and collectivities who are determined to find a way out of this problem. And they probably have still got time to do it.

The time scale is short historically but it's probably in the order of twenty years. They have probably twenty years in which to find a way out of this mess. Today we shouldn't be looking for more than the beginnings of their attempt at getting out, because it's only in the last ten years that the nature of the mess has been fully understood and is beginning to be analysed. It would be possible to point to the beginnings of these trends; the beginnings of this turning away from the acceptance of the orthodoxies of the western world or, I may add, of the eastern world as well: the beginnings of an attempt to decolonise the political cultures of the Africans to the extent of their being able to select those instrumentalities, those ideas, those technologies which they think will be useful to them, and to fit these into a synthesis

which, coming back to what we were saying earlier, also comes
out of their own roots.

*Quite simply, what did the Africans learn from their past through
different phases of colonisation and by the interaction with the
western world?*

I'm not sure one can offer a sensible answer to that. What have
we in Europe learned from our past? Well, if we've learned
anything (in the sense we're discussing here), it's that the removal
of social misery depends upon social action, collective action.
Even the most determined "individualists" don't really deny that
now: they too abound in plans and programmes which suppose
collective social and political action, even while they are assuring
us that more "individualism" — more "free enterprise", as it's
called — is the only "answer". Much like the ideas that derive
from Marx. Even our most orthodox "political scientists" draw
copiously on the ideas that derive from Marx while attacking
anybody who publicly says that the modern world can't be
understood *without* the ideas of Marx. We have a lot of "sur-
reptitious Marxists" in England. You find the same thing in
Africa: even more so. If the central lesson that Africans have
learned from the past 50 years or so is that they have to produce
their own salvation out of their own roots, there are still a lot of
leading persons who say one thing and mean another. Most of
them are part of an effort to confuse the issue, to sidetrack
revolutionary conclusions into harmless dead-ends. So you have,
in Kenya today, a country whose ruling group is entirely devoted
to "building capitalism" to its own sectional advantage — and yet
whose "ruling philosophy", as set forth in portentous documents,
is "African socialism". The idea behind "African socialism" —
in so far as there is any sincerity — seems to be that there is
something about being black that lifts you out of the laws of
history. By some magical procedure, it appears, Africa will
achieve "socialism" by a simple process of prolonging a para-
capitalist form of class exploitation. But it's also an interesting
fact that you will no longer hear such delusions presented as
serious argument by any serious person, at least not on any serious
occasion. The intellectual scene has moved on, and often moved
on quite a long way, from the debates even of ten or fifteen
years ago.

You mentioned earlier that one of the major drawbacks of the African situation is the institutional weakness which comes from different historical experiences throughout the continent. Can we place this in a wider historical perspective by making comparisons with our own experiences in both achievement and failure?

I should like to discuss the problem of nationalism a little later. Meanwhile, we can state that the problem is in any case difficult. Pre-colonial Africa was divided into many hundred more or less independent communities, most of which could reasonably be called states. Along comes the colonial period and they are all shoved together into something like 50 colonies. The only way to get rid of colonial control is to accept and use the instrument of nationalism, so we have give or take 50 colonies transformed into some 50 nation states. 50 nation states, note, not yet 50 nations. It takes time to build a nation. The Africans therefore are stuck with this situation and have to make sense of their continent from the basis of beginning from 50 or so nation-states. The orthodox formula put forward and accepted in the period of the first decolonisation in the 1950s and early 1960s was that there is no real problem. You accept the nation-state and Nigeria becomes a nation-state, Ghana becomes a nation-state etc., etc. Each one, as Rostow said in his *Stages of Economic Growth,* develops from one stage to another; it goes through an industrial revolution; the industrial revolution leads to a take off into high mass consumption, and everybody is happy. Well, it didn't work. And it didn't work because of all the reasons we've been discussing, above all the exploitative nature of the relationships between these nation states and the outside world. Also, because the institutional structures were of that nature, power fell into the hands of small ruling groups, and these small ruling groups were obliged to grow into middle classes if they were going to become bourgeoisies: if they were going to follow the formula which they had been given. In order to grow into middle classes they had to go through a process of primitive accumulation, should we say 'theft', just like the British bourgeoisie, like the French bourgeoisie, no doubt just like any other bourgeoisie – a long period of organised and systematic theft supported of course by the law. This is how capitalism is built. It's not built by democracy. The nice idea that capitalism grows together with

democracy or out of democracy is of course a myth I needn't
enlarge on here. Consequently, the new ruling groups are all
trying to become middle classes and have to do that by a process
of deliberate exploitation of the mass of their own people.
Because their developmental situation demands it, this has a
crudity like that of England in the 18th century. Naturally, they
become extremely unpopular. Since we are not in the 18th
century any longer, they can't stay in power by parliamentary
means because the masses who don't agree to being exploited
have the power to affect the state. So what happens? The military
wing of the ruling groups comes in and we get a whole succession of
military regimes simply holding the ring so that nothing can
change, and stagnation sets in. I don't want to say, incidentally,
that all the military regimes fall into that pattern because there
are interesting and important exceptions which we can talk
about later, for example in Somalia and to some extent in Nigeria.
But broadly speaking this is the situation. You can't govern by
parliamentary rule, so you govern by military dictatorship. It
has happened elsewhere.

You could even make a very crude comparison if you like
with Louis Napoleon, the second Empire in France, or with
Monsieur Guizot, his minister of finance, who said 'Enrichissez
vous', get rich, get on with it. He said this to the emergent ruling
bourgeoisie and they had the strength to do it. But Africa is not
the same. There's no emergent bourgeoisie in Africa which can
repeat the middle-class formative process which enabled a mature
capitalism to grow in Europe. That's impossible. So you simply
"hold the ring", which might be all very well if it were not for the
factors that we've been talking about; a steady impoverishment,
and therefore a constant boiling, sizzling, and heaving, with
consequently an ever greater use of force. Along this line, there is
no other way. The reason why one can still retain a relative
optimism is that new trends begin to question this whole process.
New analysis begins to penetrate its meaning so that the aware-
ness, the consciousness, of their own situation becomes stronger
in widening circles of African thought. This is very clear indeed if
you consider the student population in universities which are
becoming larger and larger. There are now fourteen universities in
Nigeria. They opened four more two or three years ago. These
students are in a situation in which they have accepted indepen-

dence as being given and have recognised the very real gains which their fathers and they themselves have benefited from. But now they are looking at the losses and are asking how to cancel these out and move forward to a new synthesis. Maybe Africa is going to move into terrible and dramatic situations, but maybe it will find the synthesis that can save it. If you look carefully at what is going on in the interstices of African life today, you find that antidotes are being produced to offset the poison deriving from the inadequate structures and ideas which often still dominate the scene.

Talking about historical parallels and points of comparison, you also make reference in your latest book to the breaking up of the Austro-Hungarian Empire after World War I into a series of new nation-states. In that case the fragmentation and subsequent creation of separate national entities came from a much larger unit, a previous political totality. Imperialism and colonialism certainly exerted a pervasive influence in Africa but could never claim a comparable geographical continuity or central administration, or to have even tried to establish one. Could you enlarge upon this point?

"Inter-continental" parallels may risk confusion, of course, just because, as you rightly insist, circumstances have differed. For me, at least (perhaps it's because of my own background of development) there are certain parallels between the decolonisation of, for example, the Austro-Hungarian Empire, and the decolonisation of Africa that have been, and remain, vividly instructive. Consider only Yugoslavia. Up to 1918 the Austrians ruled Slovenia and Bosnia, and the Hungarians ruled Croatia and the largely Serbian Vojvodina. There were differences of style and emphasis between Austrian and Hungarian colonial rule; but, as with the various empires in Africa, the essential content was pretty much the same. Then came the collapse of the Central Powers, and the emergence of the Triune Kingdom of the Serbs, Croats and Slovenes: of Yugoslavia, the country of the "south Slavs". Yugoslavia accepted the model of the bourgeois nation-state as its instrument of independence and development; but it had no established bourgeoisie, or none, at least, strong enough to exercise hegemony by the processes of parliamentary rule. So very soon there emerged a military dictatorship consisting of the king, his

generals, and various members of a commercial bourgeoisie whose
ambition was to grow, within the shelter of that dictatorship, into
an established, capital-investing, and autonomous bourgeoisie.
It was just as in Africa and, just as in Africa, it didn't work.
That was because the economic posture of that Yugoslavia was
"neo-colonial" vis-à-vis Germany, France, and Britain. We didn't
have the term "neo-colonial" in those days, but it fits exactly.
The result was that when Yugoslavia was invaded by the Axis
powers in 1941 (and I happened to be there at the time) the
country simply fell apart. The national question, in short, had
not been solved: it had only been made worse. So the task
for the Yugoslavs, fighting for their independence in a war of
liberation, was to find a viable alternative. They found this
alternative in the policies of the national liberation movement
led by Tito. Whatever failings the Yugoslav revolution may be
thought to have since then, one thing seems certain: the Yugoslav
revolution has indeed solved the national question. The solution
may not be complete, but no such problems are solved "completely". Yet it has been sufficient to push the Yugoslav national
question right off the scene of action, to settle with that question.
This was possible because the Yugoslavs, while taking experience
from the world revolutionary tradition, nevertheless worked
within the framework of their own realities. They built an indigenous synthesis. They constructed their own model, even
though, during the liberation war, they might have found it very
hard to tell you just what this model was going to be. Today,
because they did this, with whatever shortenings you may find,
it remains a sure and most creative fact that Yugoslavia has
become as different from the Yugoslavia of the Triune Kingdom
as day is different from night.

If you were to ask for "the proof in reverse", consider the
opposite experience of Greece. The Greeks also set out, during
the war, to build an alternative model to their "neo-colonial"
situation of the '20s and '30s. For whatever reasons, internal as
well as external, they failed. They were forced back into another
version of the model they had rejected. We know the results of
that: fruitless upheavals, new dictatorships, a continued spawning
of "neo-colonial" misery. In another dimension, consider the case
of Czechoslovakia. Their attempt to build an alternative model
(I am jumping a lot of history here) seems to have ended very

sadly with the totally deplorable invasion of 1968, and the subsequent effort to build a Soviet model there: does anyone seriously imagine that what is happening in Czechoslovakia today is any kind of working-out of the history and culture of the Czechs and Slovaks? On the contrary it seems much more like an interlude of frustration and stagnation: allowing for obvious differences, one might well call it a neo-colonial interlude on the African pattern.

Putting the main problem – nationalism – into an historical perspective with reference to recent events in Europe, helps our understanding considerably. But one of the things that stands out, and is an absolute priority in some cases, is the question of frontiers. What are we to make of all these claims and counter-claims that consume so much time and strength on the road to development? Are we witnessing here, in the problem of the boundaries between states, inherited as they are from colonial divisions, the beginnings of a continuing series of local wars?

The Africans themselves, their best leaders, have always been acutely aware of the problems which the frontiers in Africa now pose for them. The reasons are obvious. The frontiers were drawn not in accordance with African interests but in terms of European interests: by agreements and compromises made between the European imperial powers, mostly between 1890 and 1901, at the time of the colonial share-out. Many of the frontiers were no more than lines on the map of a continent whose geography wasn't even known, and made very little sense from any point of view, whether social, political or cultural or certainly economic. If one were to think of only one example, an extreme example but one which proves the general case, it's that of The Gambia. The Gambia in West Africa became a British colony some 400 km long but less than 100 km broad because the British wished to deny to the French the lower and middle reaches of The Gambia river, the mouth of the river. In terms of a political and economic entity The Gambia can be said to make no historical sense at all, but it is now an independent country and it is likely to remain one because the frontiers have been there for more than a hundred years. They can't simply be wished away, they are part of the given situation that Africans have to confront and will increasingly have to confront. We ought to understand that this European share-out, this part of the heritage imposed upon the Africans, forms one of their major problems — it's certainly not their fault that they have frontier problems. Let us move on to your second question: What it is going to happen in the future? I have argued in a recent book *(Africa in Modern History)* that an indefinite prolongation of nation-state nationalism on the capitalist model in Africa cannot reasonably expect to have a destiny any different in kind (however different in circumstance) from that same nationalism in Europe. Like causes produce like effects, and it is sentimental to think otherwise.

In 1964, at the height of the first phase of decolonisation, you wrote a book called Which Way Africa? *in which you analysed the roots of modern African nationalism, the complexion of the emergent nations and their perspectives. In that book, I may add, you also registered your passionate belief in independence and your participation in the ongoing process of emancipation. At that time you stressed the problems which were beginning to appear and described them as the questions of* change *and* choice. *Conditions are different but similar problems seem to need urgent consideration now. Are we on the threshhold of another crucial moment?*

That particular book was written in 1963, and published in 1964 as you say, and attempted in a simple way to sum up the achievements of the nationalist struggles in Africa which resulted in the first de-colonisations of the late '50s and early '60s. That was a period when one was still, as it were, absorbing the results, the achievements of those de-colonisations; but also when one was beginning to see the size of the price that Africans had to pay for accepting the institutional models within which they had received their independence. The book was called *Which Way Africa?* but I don't pretend that it gave any clear answers as to which way Africa was really going. We re-published in 1967 and 1971 in subsequently revised editions and came a little nearer to answering the question in the title. But I think the answer to your point about a "new threshold" is both yes and no. No, because it is quite evident that the process of finding indigenous solutions to the kind of problems which have arisen from the first de-colonisations is going to be a long one. One shouldn't see it as a moment or a short period in time, but as a more or less long period of transition. But yes, on the other hand, we *are* at a "new threshold" because now it is very clear that the existing structures and systems don't work and that alternatives *have* to be found. The general problem today is therefore substantially different from that of twenty years ago. Twenty years ago it was a matter of getting rid of the colonial system in order to work out indigenous solutions. The problem now, twenty years later, precisely is to elaborate those solutions, and apply them.

III

African Reform and the Alternatives

I would like to draw together some of the threads and summarise what we have been saying.

We have said

1. that one of the major gains of the period of decolonisation over the past 30 years has been and remains a new understanding, never available before, of African history, and hence of African realities;

2. that this must also be seen as one of the main gains of a political decolonisation which also exacted a price, even a heavy price;

3. that the price paid for those political and cultural gains, as shown by upheavals and disasters on every side in Africa at the moment, now begins to appear larger than the gains. This, I suggest, is merely an appearance – largely promoted by the provincial vulgarity of our mass media – an appearance persuasive only to those who have forgotten, or never known, just how stagnant and constricting the colonial systems really were;

4. that, in any case, the failure of the institutional model of the capitalist nation-state is now such that any further prolongation of its trends – notably the inherent failure of productive systems to supply the needs of rapidly growing populations – can only threaten grave disasters in the next twenty years or so.

Shall we now see how the old model can be overcome and on what foundations the new one may be sustained and strengthened?
It's part of a debate which is now in full course in Africa, at least among progressive-thinking Africans, especially among young Africans; and we can I think draw from that debate a number of conclusions. It's clear that any alternative model, if it is to be

workable and fruitful, will have to be a model which, while taking ideas and technologies from the outside world, nonetheless remains, organically, a *development* of previous African history. It must be firstly a development out of, and also to some extent against, the precolonial heritage: that is, all those precolonial models within which the Africans used to live in times often called "traditional". Second it must be a development out of, and most certainly against, the colonial heritage: that is, the heritage of the bourgeois nation-state in its form, institutionally, structurally, transferred to Africa.

This is not, of course, saying anything particularly new or surprising. You will find such conclusions widely held in Africa today. Nor is it saying anything that is especially "historicist", although personally I think that the admitted "subjectivity of historicism" is vastly to be preferred, because vastly less misleading, than the supposed "neutrality" of those who claim that history has no pattern, no processual movement, no logical development: in short, displays and can display no progress. For if it is not conceived as process, then history is what Henry Ford said it was: history is bunk, or, at best, an intellectual amusement, a cultural decoration. But if history is a process then it has to be understood as process, and explained as such. And in this context the history of modern Africa is the process of development (transition, if you prefer) from pre-colonial structures, cultures and institutions to fully modernising structures, cultures and institutions, capable of meeting problems and challenges of today, which are altogether different from those of a hundred years ago.

The colonial period, in European mythology, was supposed to have effected that particular transition. Generally, however, it did nothing of the kind. Historically, from this standpoint, the colonial period was a hiatus, a standstill, an interlude when African history was stopped or was forced to become, for that period, a part of European history.

Having reached this point in our discussion, we also reach a major question. What alternative model of development is possible? What effective forms can or does the further unfolding of African history now reveal?

Two preliminary points here . . .

1. We are not concerned with fake alternatives which are merely a facade for the defence of privileged ruling groups who continue their own history of primitive accumulation at the expense of the majority. The verbiage of "African socialism" need not detain us, nor any of its simulacra. On the contrary, we are concerned with that development of Africa's social history in which, within the context of our world today, power passes from the few to the many, from the rulers to the masses. We are concerned, in short, with a very specific class struggle.

2. It will be well to avoid any theorising in the abstract. It may be that a viable Marxist theory of structural change in Africa will emerge in the next twenty years or so: that Marxism, applied as an analysis of African reality and *within* African reality, will produce in time a body of appropriate doctrine applicable to all African situations. Perhaps that will be so but it is not so now. Most Marxist analyses of African structural process (and, we may note, non-Marxist ones even more) are up to now far too deeply marked by ethno-centrism to have much value. African Marxism, freed of that non-African ethno-centrism, is still a new enterprise, dating perhaps only to the work in the 1960s of such outstanding thinkers as the late Amilcar Cabral. That is in no way to say. let me add, that Marxist analyses of *particular* segments of African reality, of the *here* and of the *now,* are not already a very valid enterprise. We already owe a great deal of enlightenment to African and non-African Marxists working in particular situations.

Yet one or two general observations may still be permissible.

The accepted model of the capitalist nation-state, as we see it stumbling along in Africa today, manifestly does not meet the needs of structural and cultural development. Telescoping the argument, for the purposes of our discussion, we can safely affirm that the capitalist model cannot in any case meet those needs.

Why Not?

The central reason why it cannot meet those needs — cannot even defend itself effectively — is to be found in the class structure of these countries. With one or two exceptions, they reached independence without an established bourgeoisie. Therefore, in order to make the capitalist model work, they have to build an established bourgeoisie, a bourgeoisie capable of exercising its hegemony at every decisive point of control, direct or indirect. But they cannot build this bourgeoisie because the economic relationship between Africa and the rest of the world — with the so-called *developed* world, that is — remains one of dependence. All they can build are subsidiary bourgeoisies, auxiliary bourgeoisies, what Africans generally call "neo-colonial" bourgeoisies. The process of wealth transfer overseas continues. Meanwhile the process of trying to build indigenous bourgeoisies meets the rising challenge of great majorities who clamour against falling living standards, stagnant conditions of life, growing shortages of food and everyday necessities, and the rest. With one or two conceivable exceptions — and the exceptions, if they occur, will only prove the rule (Nigeria may be one of them) — it is too late in history to build an indigenous capitalism in Africa. The existing systems may grow in gross annual output: they cannot develop, on this model, from dependent systems into self-generating and self-reliant systems.

This being evidently the case — and I know of no evidence which can affirm the contrary outside the realm of capitalist propaganda — then the only possible alternative model has to be non-capitalist.

What do you mean by that?

Yes, what is non-capitalist? What is the socialism to which it is claimed that a non-capitalist alternative will lead? What, if any, are the universalist points of reference that emerge in this context? Where and how does the non-African revolutionary experience — the whole body of experience reaching back to the eighteenth century in Europe, even to the seventeenth in the case of England — find its links with the African realities we understand today so much better than we understood them thirty years ago?

Such questions, as I said earlier, can usefully be considered, at least at this stage of history, in concrete cases, in actual realities, rather than in any attempt to abstract an "all-purpose" theory.

Could you give me some concrete examples?

The best African thinkers of these recent years have avoided any such abstraction. Cabral, for example, almost never spoke of socialism in relation to the programme of the PAIGC in Guinea-Bissau*; or even of non-capitalism. The programme and policies of the PAIGC, today as yesterday, are certainly non-capitalist and certainly within the arena of socialist thought and practice. But to speak of socialism is to speak of a system and relations of production, a cultural level of literacy and understanding, which the society of Guinea-Bissau has yet to win. They are objectives for a more or less long future. One may believe that this is the only future that is worth working for — the leaders of the PAIGC have certainly believed that in the past and believe it today — but meanwhile, as Cabral used to insist, it is necessary not to confuse the ideas which you have in your head with the realities within which you live. For if you do not make that distinction you will fall into demagogy, and if you fall into demagogy you will not be believed, and if you are not believed you will not be followed.

Even so, one may offer one or two generalisations that may be useful at least in terms of explanation. One of them concerns the vital necessity of *mass participation*. Now there is a demagogy of mass participation, and it does its part in adding to confusion. But there is also — and we can discuss it in concrete African examples — a *practice* of mass participation. This practice, as observable in the genuinely revolutionary movements in Africa today — and they exist in more countries than the mass media will generally care to admit — has derived not from any demagogy, but from the very process and development of a class as well as national struggle.

The liberation movements in the Portuguese colonies, for example, were obliged by Salazarist intransigence to declare armed warfare on the colonial system. They had no other choice. Either they surrendered, or they fought. Either they won, or they would be destroyed to the last militant. But in order to fight, and certainly in order to win, they were then obliged to develop a mass participation. Those who began were few, often very few

---

*PAIGC: African Independence Party of Guinea-Bissau (formerly Portuguese Guinea) and Cape Verde. Formed in 1956, this party fought its way to the independence of these two Portuguese territories in 1974-75.

— only six men, in the case of the PAIGC when it was founded in 1956 — and they could not hope to fight, much less to win, merely on the basis of mass support, goodwill, sympathy, applause. They could not, in other words, hope to succeed as merely populist movements, instruments of propaganda for reformist pressure, relying on big words, bigger promises, or any of the apparatus of demagogic agitation. If they won only mass sympathy — and that wasn't in any case too difficult to secure, given the severe repressions and exactions of the Portuguese colonial system — then they faced defeat and death: and both defeat and death, in that case, would be certain.

So what was their main problem?

Their essential problem, then, was to develop mass support into mass participation. It was an enormously difficult but unavoidable problem, with its solution the only possible road to success, the only possible method of giving to liberation a meaning worthy of the word. In these circumstances of a necessary armed struggle against colonial violence, their problem had already been defined by a Vietnamese revolutionary, Nguyen Van Tien. He said that: "What has to be achieved is that people *themselves* discover the need for armed struggle. As for guns, those you can always find . . ." And here, if you will allow me an aside, one sees very clearly indeed the difference between an armed struggle for liberation and the individualist opportunism, or worse, of those who embark on the terrorism that Europe now sees. The object of terrorism is not to win mass support, much less mass participation: it is to use terror in order to *impose* the control of a minority, even of a contemptibly small minority, on the life of the majority. The ideology and morality of armed struggle for liberation has no relationship, save one of complete opposition, with the ideology and morality of terrorism. To confuse the two is to fall into the worst of provincial errors, or merely, of course, to become the deluded victim of a criminal conspiracy.

And what do you make of the present situation?

It seems to me, if an Englishman may say it, that Italians at any rate have the least possible excuse for falling into that error, for misunderstanding the difference between counter-violence used by mass participation in structural change, and terror used as the weapon of a mere adventure. No doubt the history of Italy is indeed very different from the history of Mozambique: no doubt the circumstances of Nazi-occupied Italy in 1943-45 were very different from those of colonial Mozambique twenty years later. All the same, the need to win mass participation in the fight of the Resistance, and even the very process of winning it, were essentially the same in kind as the comparable need and process in the Mozambique that FRELIMO eventually liberated from colonial rule.

Don't you think that this comparison may seem a bit far-fetched?

It may sound a little shocking to ethnoc-centric ears. It nonetheless remains true. I think back myself to the case of Liguria where I had the good fortune to serve for a little while. In central Liguria, where I arrived in January 1945, large regions had been liberated by the partisan divisions and lesser units of the Sixth Zone, as it was then called. These divisions were composed of volunteers who were the fruit of having won a mass participation in that struggle since September 1943: just as, alongside them, the men and women who formed committees of national liberation in countless places were another fruit of that same successful process. But how had those divisions and brigades begun? Where was their origin? In the case of the Sixth Zone, of the partisans who liberated Genoa before the Allies came on the scene, the origins lay in a handful of men, the "band of Cichero" raised by G.B. Canepa and his comrades. They too were very few: and if I am not wrong, at Christmas time of 1943 they numbered only six persons − exactly like the PAIGC in 1956. But they went on to win because they were able to set in motion the whole process of winning mass participation: *not* merely mass support, please note, *not* the mere agreement or sympathy of a population, but the real and active participation in that struggle of men and women of all ages, beliefs, and anti-fascist opinions.

My point here is still a general one, but I think essential. How did Canepa and his comrades win that mass participation? By terror? Not in the least: no such terror was thinkable, and even if it had been thinkable it would have failed. By demagogy? But what demagogy could prevail against Nazi and Blackshirt firing squads and torture cells? No, they won it by the practice of a democratic alternative. It was the only way; and it was out of that practice that there developed a most objective conviction of a necessary and indispensable link between democracy and revolutionary change — a conviction which has steered the best of political thought and practice in Italy (for example) ever since.

How can a democratic alternative be envisaged in concrete terms in Africa today?

The reason for referring here to that link between democracy and socialism is that it has a precise and direct application to any understanding of the possible alternative in Africa today. Only an alternative model capable of developing that link can be a model capable of solving, as we have indeed seen in the concrete examples of the Portuguese colonies, the real and actual problems of the Africans in this period of their history: or, for all I know, in any future period. The democracy of mass participation is the only effective mode of revolution in our time, and the only effective guarantee of revolution in our day: outside that equation, all the rest is peripheral, subordinate, or merely demagogic. The anti-fascist struggle and the anti-colonial struggle find their common harvest here.

And the problem is how to keep the momentum of mass participation from the liberation struggle of yesterday to the tasks of recovery and development of tomorrow. How to move on, in other words, to what one may call a higher stage, that of structural change.

That is completely true. I agree with that entirely. But it is from the basis of that particular question that you raise, and perhaps only on the basis of that particular question, that one can go on to examine the whole problematic of African revolutionary change. The liberation movements, whether or not by armed struggle each according to its different circumstances and possible options, bring states into being by the process of mass participation. These states are the instruments of the movements in question. Their regimes, to quote here the latest analytical self-analysis of the PAIGC, are "liberation movements in power". But what, after liberation, is the relationship between state and party? What forms of the *mediation of power,* of state power, government power, party power, are to ensure the further health and development of the mass participation which brought these parties and states into existence? What structural modes of operation can broaden and deepen the practice of democracy? What can prevent the ossification of party power, the bureaucratisation of revolutionary committees, administrations, initiatives — the rise of new kinds of "self-perpetuating élites"?

Now I pose these questions not because the answers are fully known, but rather because they are now in process of being found and applied: in Mozambique, for instance, from which I have just returned. They are exactly the questions with which the best revolutionaries in Africa now are wrestling every day.

Having succeeded so far, how can they continue that success? They are into a terrain for which there is no clear answer from any revolutionary experience that we have yet assembled. There are no guarantees. But after all you don't set out on a process of liberation after receiving guarantees that you will infallibly succeed. You have to solve new problems as you go along.

No doubt the general answer, the textbook answer, is perfectly obvious: you prevent the rise of new kinds of self-perpetuating élites by reinforcing, expanding, developing those very processes of mass participation which you set in motion during the struggle, and which made anti-colonial liberation possible.

But how do you do this?

That is where the drama lies — and not, as you rightly say, by any means only an African drama. Perhaps it is even the central challenge to Marxist thought today? We lack, or so it seems to me, an effective theory of the state in this stage of the transition from capitalist anarchy, quite apart from whatever the state may be found to be, when eventually we reach socialism! Some have blamed Soviet Marxists for failing to come to grips with any such theory. For me that's quite unrealistic. They are evidently incapable of doing that yet, just because they are incapable, so far as one can see, of reaching an analysis of the Stalinist phenomenon in more than individual or subjective terms. Perhaps they will become capable (and personally, I hope they will). But in the meantime it's a job that has to be done. There is, for example, much talk of "Leninism" in some African quarters today. But what is this "Leninism" when applied to the state, to the party, to relations between party and state? Lenin's formulations in

State and Revolution are one thing: what actually happened *after* 1917, after the civil war, after the foreign interventions, after Lenin's death — all that is quite another. Now the African revolutionary experience does in fact begin to be interesting precisely in terms of this debate.

But leaving that aside, what can one say of the political democratic practice in Africa that is beginning to appear?

Labels apart (and personally like Cabral I dislike them), what the African experience can at any rate claim to begin to show, however tentatively as yet, is a concrete experience in facing this problem of the mediation of power in certain countries which have won their independence. To this extent, the African experience reveals another onward step from the period of "classical de-colonisation", the period of the decolonisation of the late 1950s and 1960s. The old mole has tunnelled further: deviously, with enormous difficulty, often turning back in his tracks: but all the same, by and large, further. And in tunnelling further, this African experience begins to approach our own: the roads converge. All roads used to lead to Rome, they say. Then all roads were said, by some at least, to lead to Moscow, or, of course, on the other side, to Washington. Today the roads of revolution, of a real development, lead to as many collectivities as there are national states: but they lead, even so, ever more closely to the same conclusions. It is another of the dialectical ironies of history, but a pleasant one this time.

Different countries in Africa have achieved their independence in different ways and perhaps contrasting roads to freedom and progress follow from this. In the case of the Portuguese colonies, for instance, the people liberated themselves and, in so doing, have possibly gone deeper into the task of progressive structural changes and actual emancipation from past and present colonialism, laying the foundations of a non-capitalist system. Is there a different outcome in other cases where independence was granted or reached in less painful circumstances? It is obviously not possible to guarantee that subsequent progress will be a democratic, participatory exercise; but can we identify certain preconditions that will make it more likely that what takes place afterwards will respond in the most appropriate way to the needs of that particular country and its people?

Let's come down to the concrete realities of one or two cases: having cleared the ground of a number of preliminary or theoretical considerations, we can now make a little investigation. If you look for instance at what's happening in the Portuguese colonies which you mentioned, in the territories which are now liberated (Guinea-Bissau, Angola and Mozambique, Cape Verde and São Tomé), you will find that they are all operating on much the same basic analysis and policy. This analysis and policy, historically, are in their style and in some of their basic ideas quite close to Lenin's formulation of 1917, in *State and Revolution*. But of course they take shape in circumstances enormously different from those of Russia in that time. And I think that one can perhaps encapsulate the argument in the following way. Liberation in those colonies resulted from the active and voluntary participation of masses of people in the liberation struggle led by the cadres, the trained militants, not very many in numbers, of the liberation movement in question, whether it was FRELIMO in Mozambique, the MPLA in Angola or the PAIGC in Guinea-Bissau and Cape Verde. And there you see evolving two basic concepts, basic approaches. One is that in order to maintain the momentum of structural change it is necessary at this point to transform a broad liberation movement into a much more closely organised and structured political party. A political party which commands the state and which guarantees, in the measure of the possible, the further unfolding of the general programme of liberation: which means, of course, the raising of the cultural, social and economic life of the masses, the long struggle to end — as they argue — the exploitation of man by man. That's one aspect of it. It is very necessary and very difficult because 85 to 90% of the population of those countries are rural people, not only illiterate but pre-literate, with very small experience of the outside world and, let us remember, with no experience at all in self-government since the colonial system began to be imposed upon them many decades ago. Since the colonial systems were outright dictatorships, the need is to transform the state from an outright dictatorship into a democratic state. I refer back to the link between democracy and revolutionary change. The liberation movement becomes a much more organised and structured party of militants who are trained both politically and technologically in order to steer the state, to steer society, along its route to development. Good: but how they do you prevent that party from becoming a self-perpetuating élite? How do you prevent the increasing bureaucratisation of life in Angola, Mozambique and Guinea-Bissau?

There you meet the second basic concept which takes shape, and that is the reinforcement of the process of mass participation. They call it the development of *poder popular,* people's power. This notion of people's power takes shape at various levels. It takes shape in a large extension of local government in the hands of local assembles, village assemblies, district assemblies, town assemblies, each with its own executives, to which more and more responsibilities are handed in the measure that they are able to handle them. That is a small measure in many cases to begin with, though often a large measure in those areas which were liberated during the struggle, where local committees of self-government, already even at the beginning of the 1970s, had quite extensive forms of democratic self-rule in action. The problem has been to extend those structures from the old liberated zones, as they are called, into zones which were liberated from the Portuguese at the end of the war 1974-75. The solution is *poder popular.*

Secondly it takes the form of promoting trade union structures where none existed. No trade union existed in the Portuguese colonies, save the shadow of corporative trade unions on the fascist model, and those only for Europeans. Accordingly there is now a big effort to form trade unions, which you will find in all the countries I have mentioned. You will find trade unions beginning to take shape as organs for mobilising and organising workers in their work place, not only to defend their own interests but also to advance these interests by promoting better systems of production and exchange, and by ensuring the welfare of the families of the workers. You will find mass participation similarly taking shape in other forms of mass organisation, and I think here particularly of women. And of course you find the same participation taking shape in new revolutionary parties.

In all colonial countries the women were the real wretched of the earth, they were those who were most exploited. So that the woman question in Africa is one of the central issues of liberation.

Without the self-liberation of women no real progress is going to be made in terms of this reinforcement of the forms of mass participation we have been talking about. And they are well aware of this. Not long ago, actually in November 1976, there was held a remarkable meeting, one of the most interesting that there's ever been of this kind, I should think. The Mozambican Organisation of Women (OMA) called together a conference of some two hundred women each of whom had been elected by a local committee, by a local group, by a local trade union, in order to discuss the concrete issues of how women are and what they need to be in Mozambique today. It was not a general discussion at all, but very severely concrete. About half of these women were illiterate but being illiterate is no bar to understanding the world about one. If you read the proceedings of that conference, published at quite extensive length, you find a startling light being thrown upon a zone of life in Africa where nothing previously had been said outside the private circle. At this conference they talked in public, *as* women, about the exploitation of women. They talked about the problems of unmarried mothers, the problems of prostitution, the problems of divorce, the problems of wages. These were women speaking for themselves in a congress which was not simply a congress for decoration, but a congress whose resolutions then went to the government, for the government to take some action about. Now this is only one example of the way in which mass participation is being unfolded in these concrete cases. You could say much the same thing about Angola or Guinea-Bissau, where you have, for the first time in history, effective channels of communication and self expression open to wide segments of the population who never before could come out in public with their problems and discuss them.

Let me repeat: *effective* channels — that is, channels which are built in order to be operative within an overall structure, or organisation, capable of joining all these constituent persons, villages, ethnic groups, not only to each other, but also, and again in a sense never possible before, to the problems and opportunities of the modern world in relation to their own country. That is a great gain: historically, perhaps, the onset of a continental "turning point".

Then everything is solved? Not in the least. In matters of this kind there are no "final solutions", no cast-iron guarantees, nothing is automatic. All that is sure is that a turning point is reached and the road ahead becomes clear to see, if still hard to follow. If it is true that freedom has to defend itself every day if it is to survive, let alone expand, then the same is true of any genuine process of mass participation: freedom in this sense, and mass participation, are the same thing. The problems in this case — in Angola, or anywhere else in Africa now — are difficult for the theoretical reasons you have indicated: the reasons, if you like, common to human nature, to the human condition. But there are also practical reasons, among which is the unhappy fact that these countries have had to inherit at least part of a colonial bureaucracy; this bureaucracy is utterly unsuited to solving the problems of freedom and development, of freedom *in* development, because it is a bureaucracy formed in a colonial tradition of autocracy, sloth, irresponsibility and petty corruption. This means that the liberation-movement-in-power — its leadership, its best militants — have to be strong, patient and tough enough, not only to absorb the inefficiencies and irresponsibilities of that part of the bureaucracy which they have had to inherit, but also, somehow or other, to build meanwhile a new and progressive bureaucracy. That will take time, a lot of time. Just as the raising of the cultural level of the society as a whole — meaning, just as much, raising the level of political understanding, carrying society beyond its constrictive provincialism — also takes a lot of time. I don't know how much time, but I shan't, I think, be misrepresenting the best leaders of Africa today if I say that this period of structural and cultural transition — this revolutionary period, if you like — that we are now entering has to be seen in decades. Maybe around AD 2000 we can do another interview on the same lines, and draw up a "balance sheet"?

This said, I don't wish to be misunderstood. Historically, the period we are living through in Africa now is nonetheless a crucial "moment", the onset of a "turning point". Much more than during the earlier period of decolonisation, these years now are when African history begins again, comes to grips with its inner realities and starts to unfold on original lines. A major crossroads, if you like; a turning towards new directions.

So far you have been talking mainly about Angola, Mozambique and Guinea-Bissau. Could you add some other example of a

*country where mass participation and development got together
and went some way to at least begin to answer the first basic
questions?*

That brings to mind another concrete case which is perhaps more
convincing because it is easier to see, as it were, on the ground.
The liberation of women is a process which goes on within all
these societies, a long and difficult process, but often hard to see
at work. However if you go to Cape Verde archipelago today
you'll see a demonstration of this link between democracy and
revolutionary change — democracy, mass participation and
development — actually unfolding on the ground. The Cape
Verde archipelago, ten islands, three hundred and twenty thousand
people, six hundred km out into the Atlantic, has been an independent state since 1975. Yet it is so unknown to the outside world
that it might have come out of the sea. In fact, needless to say,
it's always been out there, populated since the 16th century
as a Portuguese colony. It's in the same latitude as the African
Sahara and it suffers from the same very severe droughts from
time to time, cyclical droughts which strike the Cape Verde
islands every twenty or thirty years and often last for several
years. It happens that the worst and latest of these cyclical
droughts began in 1969 and continued until 1978. So that the
people of the Cape Verde islands, led by the PAIGC in the Cape
Verde, inherited not only a colonial situation, they also inherited
a very severe drought.

Now the Portuguese colonial rulers, during those years of
drought, had been shamed into admitting its existence. Having
done that, they felt obliged to do something to relieve its consequences. But what *could* they do, as a colonial power? It's an
instructive example. Like other colonial powers in comparable
situations, they could not help the people to help themselves:
because once people are helped to help themselves, then people
begin to act independently, think independently — become, in
short, "trouble-makers" in the jargon of colonial rule. So the
colonial rulers were forced back on charity — on the sort of
paternalist benevolence which could, it is true, help a little to
relieve the worst consequences of this particular drought, but in
no way help the people of Cape Verde to change their own
realities. They handed out money in charity. Some roads useful
to the Portuguese army were built, but nothing was done that

could contribute towards changing the ecology of the Cape Verdes: because changing the ecology must have meant changing the society — and that would have spelt "trouble" It was the usual colonial case.

However the new rulers of 1975 — the PAIGC voted into power by an overwhelming majority of votes in June 1975: and in an election, sceptics should note, supervised *by* the still existing colonial authorities — were in an entirely different case. Their whole policy rested on helping the people to help themselves, on handing out responsibility to the people, on changing the realities of Cape Verde. They could have no fear of "trouble-makers": on the contrary, the "trouble" so greatly feared by the colonial rulers was precisely what they most wished to promote. They entirely reversed colonial policy: in this instance, on the problems of cyclical drought. They asked for emergency aid from abroad — from the United Nations, from any country that would give such aid without tieing strings to it — and in fact they received, in comparative terms, quite a lot of such aid.

But they didn't hand it out in charity, they didn't hand it out in queues to the unemployed. They mobilised the people through their committees to build very many kms of water-retaining dykes, to build many wells, to build a whole system of water retention in exchange for wages which derived from this foreign aid. So that when this drought ends, the rain will not fall upon the Cape Verdes and pour off into the Ocean as it always has in the past but a proportion of it, perhaps even a large proportion of rainfall, will actually be retained on the islands. It is a very simple case, but it has been done by mobilising the unity and energy of Cape Verdian people. If you look at the island of Fogo, "the fire", an extraordinary island, a volcano rising three thousand meters out of the sea in a great cone and still active from time to time with a population of about forty thousand people, you will find that these people have been mobilised, have mobilised themselves through their own committees, their own assemblies, to build scores of kms of dykes, water protection walls. These works don't make much difference at the moment, because the rain is still not there. But when the rain falls on Fogo then this potentially very fertile island, covered in volcanic ash as it is, capable of growing all sorts of fruit, coffee, wine, peaches, pears, applies, will have reservoirs of water which can at least lessen the effects of droughts in the future. I give that simply as a concrete case of what it means when a people is mobilised to change its own realities.

That kind of emergency in an isolated and extraordinary place is a special situation, but it can be taken to indicate, and not only symbolically, a larger and harder task in all emergent societies. That is how to retain a sense of urgency among the people, a mass determination to change the shape of things in ordinary and extremely varied situations of everyday life where the risk is that, as time progresses, not only the will to radically alter the structures but the productivity rate also might begin to falter. The objective and the degree of its success would then be measured by the government's ability to maintain the maximum sense of urgency and range of popular participation.

The risk is always there: only utopians can think that humanity ever solves its problems "once and for all'. But in any case, and in general, this is all an "extraordinary situation". This is an emergency and the emergency continues. The liberation wars may be over: but the problems are just as difficult, acute, tense in their psychological dimensions — perhaps more so. That's another thing that people in Europe tend to overlook. There's no African country whose real condition today, admitted or not, is less than one of profound crisis. The challenge of that crisis isn't over: on the contrary, it's part of the daily scene. Let me offer you another "concrete case" of what I mean.

In Angola there is a large Atlantic port called Lobito. It possesses among other things the biggest floating-dock for ship repair on the whole west coast, south of Nigeria anyway. This dock was constructed and floated by the Portuguese in 1969. It was never repainted, and never beached for overhaul. By 1975, when independence came, this dock was in very bad condition. Threatened with collapse through lack of overhaul, its loss would mean the loss of many jobs. So it had to be beached for overhaul, and as a matter of urgency. But who was going to undertake this difficult technical job, and carry it through with some hope of success? A tough question. Lobito had had 230 skilled ship-repair workers before independence. They were all Portuguese, and within a month of independence, all but four of them had quit the country, panicked by their own leaders into going back to Portugal.

That left some 400 Angolan ship-repair workers. But none of these had been trained or paid as skilled workers: colonial-fashion, they were the "assistants" of the Portuguese skilled workers. Many of them had in fact done skilled work; all the same, none of them had had the chance to develop their skills or acquire a corresponding level of responsibility.

Here indeed was Africa's crisis in miniature. Something had to be done, but there was no one of recognised competence to do it. Elsewhere they might have sat down and waited for foreign experts. Not here, not in this liberated country. The new national-ised management and its trade union committee told me what they did. They called a meeting of their Angolan ship-repair workers and discussed the situation. It was decided to take the risk, technically a big one, and beach the floating dock, overhaul it, and float it again. I remember the leading cadre's words to me: "We got the dock out of the water in 48 hours, working round the clock. Then we scoured and painted it, and we got it safely back into the water within one month". That was in February 1977; in May, when I was there, the dock was about to take its first ship for major repairs. The dock was saved; so were the jobs.

Now this is the kind of emergency that is real in people's minds, the kind of solution that really educates. Not many people outside Lobito heard about the dock crisis and its solution, but inside Lobito they were talking of little else for months. It is an example, even a small example, but you could generalise it for Africa. Wherever such crises are solved in such ways, things change. Wherever they are not, despair grows. Either way, you are up against emergency. Of course we can't know how this emergency will be met, in the future, in all those countries where radical ideas, revolutionary approaches, are still to be developed, or are now repressed by the neo-colonial state.

Nobody can say exactly what shape things will take in the future because the new reality is the product of the free interplay of forces in society, the proper dialectics of liberation. But we have established that positive elements towards the building of an alternative model are in fact the intensification of democratic struggles and mass participation. What about those countries

which inherited forms of western style parliamentary democracy?
Have they achieved their independence in a less painful but also
less fruitful way in the long run?

It seems to me that you could make a very interesting contrast
between Kenya and Tanzania. Both achieved their independence
by a process of compromise and were presented with the par-
liamentary model on the best pattern of Westminster. Each was
sent a large wig for the speaker and a handsome mace for the
"sergeant-at-arms" and was instructed on the rules of debate
according to the best model of Erskine May in the Parliament
of Britain. Nonetheless these two countries have taken very
different roads.

We can say rather little about that here, it's very complex. In
Kenya the official programme of the ruling party, effectively
the only party, is called "African Socialism". This is a mythical
concept, and to be sharply distinguished from the original forms
of socialism which may emerge in due course in the specific
circumstances of Africa. In actual fact, what happens in Kenya
is the growth of an auxiliary bourgeoisie vowed to building, in
Kenya, another extension of the Western capitalist system. It is a
characteristic "neo-colonial" programme. The basic structures
and approaches of the colonial period are carried over into
independence, and modified only to the extent that *direct*
control becomes local: and is exercised, in fact, by the "elite"
leadership of an auxiliary bourgeoisie. The bulk of the usable
economic surplus, in other words, is divided between foreign
investors and this "elite"; and parliament, in so far as it functions,
becomes the monopolised instrument of a "party" which is the
tool of that elite. The latter accumulates capital, at present
largely for commerce or luxury expenditure, while the gap in
income-levels between this elite and the mass of the population
grows not narrower, as independence promised, but continually
wider.

It is a recognisable situation because this is how capitalism is
built. But can it be built in Kenya? Opinions differ. There are
those, even on the left, who believe that the present system
can in fact develop into a self-generating capitalism. There are
others, including me, who think that this is at least improbable:

because the relationship of Kenya to the Western capitalist system is such that existing processes of wealth-transfer *to* that system must continue, and, in continuing, necessarily defeat all attempts to build an indigenous — that is, self-generating — capitalist system in Kenya. It is, in short, too late in time for the building of new capitalist systems: all that can be built, today, are dependent extensions to the existing systems. In any case, in Kenya today, you have all the deepening imbalances of a system which works well only for a minority of beneficiaries, and not always well even for them.

This spectacle in Kenya was among the reasons why its neighbour to the south, Tanzania, embarked on a different direction from about 1967. In the thinking of Julius Nyerere, Tanzania's well-known leader, the "Kenya model" was going to lead to increasing strife, frustration and defeat. Another instructive case: for Nyerere had begun as a liberal and developed into what one might reasonably call a utopian socialist. Now, under various pressures, he went further. Feeling his way, and for a long time very distrustful of any Marxist analysis or approach, he developed a programme which moved from the "idealism" of "African Socialism" to a more realist plan for self-development by processes of mass participation. He was able to carry his party, the ruling Tanzanian African National Union, sufficiently with him: not without defections, need I say, and not without insincerities. It remains that the policies and socio-economic programmes of Tanzania, by 1972, had become different in principle, approach and even application, from any that had existed before 1967. Banks, insurance companies, import-export enterprises there, and other interests in foreign hands were nationalised: so, too, a little later, were most of the foreign-owned sisal plantations. Plans were put on foot to mobilise the rural communities for the self-determination of their collective lives within more rational, more technologically equipped, structures. All this was in sharp contrast to policies in Kenya. But was this more than an extension of state capitalism? Could it solve the problem of a proliferating bureaucracy — and avoid the crystallisation of a larger "ruling group", even if this group had no *direct* possession of the "commanding heights" of the economy? Could the mobilisation of the masses be in any way consistent with a stiff control of trade unions, with for example a ban on all strikes? By 1972 these had become very open questions, and the processes of mass participation were being widely undermined by bureaucratic "orders from above". With what result? Critics differ. Some think that the Tanzanian solution is only another form of neo-colonial continuity; others, to whom I tend to belong myself, think that it is going to prove, in the upshot, the beginning of a transfer of effective power to the great majority of people.

Whatever view you take, this vivid contest in Tanzania is the illustration of a large African problem. How do you find a road to socialism − to the real thing, not its mythical facade, not its bureaucratic dispossessor − out of an existing and previously accepted "neo-colonial" sub-capitalism? How do you get the petty bourgeoisie "to commit suicide as a class", as a group, in Amílcar Cabral's challenging phrase, in the interests of the rural and urban masses? How do you change the ethos, the ideology, of a ruling elite? How then do you get large masses of people on the move − when, generally, there is no acute "point of explosion", no great emergency that dramatises the need to get on the move? Well, we are aware of this problem nearer home. But just as a comparison of Kenya and Tanzania is instructive, so too in this respect is a comparison of Tanzania with its neighbour to the southward, with Mozambique.

For in Mozambique there was precisely this "point of explosion", this manifest and immediate need to build something altogether different, a state quite different from the colonial state. This was partly because the Portuguese were too weak, economically, to offer any neo-colonial model, and partly because FRELIMO, the Mozambican liberation movement, could then free the country from colonial control only by destroying the colonial system − and therefore, in any institutional sense, the basis for a neo-colonial system. FRELIMO, moreover, had its alternative model to hand. It had begun to construct that model, based on the process of evoking and promoting mass participation, in zones liberated from colonial control during the war of 1964-75. FRELIMO could and did take power not only with a clear notion and some experience of what an alternative model had to mean, but also, and decisively, with a large number of militants who shared this notion and experience.

So that the imbalances of Mozambican society today are

nothing like those now increasing in Kenya, and very little like those which have taken shape in Tanzania since 1967. The imbalances in Mozambique do not derive from a widening gap between a neo-colonial ruling group and the mass of the population, for no such gap exists; nor are they caused, save marginally, by the power of a bureaucracy schooled in the colonial tradition. The Mozambican imbalances are the fruit of a long and profound deprivation: of mass illiteracy, much poverty, economic problems unavoidably inherited from the colonial period and so on. They are precisely the imbalances which the policies and programme of FRELIMO are designed to redress and gradually remove.

So you have these instructive comparisons. This can't be any kind of catalogue, but of course the comparisons could be multiplied. Consider only the acute and most instructive comparison to be drawn between Morocco and Algeria, between Congo and Gabon, between Senegal and Guinea-Bissau, or other sets of neighbours. All of them in their different ways illustrate what I think of as the struggle between the neo-colonial consequences of the first decolonisations (of the late '50s, early '60s), and, on the other side, the striving for a second decolonisation that can carry the gains of the first decolonisation into the field of genuine all-round development.

These are the comparisons, it seems to me, that the young generations of Africans today look to for their guide on what should be done. Not that armed struggle is any necessary road to a further liberation — to what I have called, very approximately, a second decolonisation: but that a further independence, a greater independence, calls and must call for revolutionary change. This may exact a price, but there may be no way to avoid paying it. Where armed struggle has been necessary, as in Mozambique, Africa's younger generations today — if one may risk so great a generalisation — almost certainly think the price was well worth paying. For if the Mozambicans have had to go through eleven years of war, savage bombing, concentration camps and the rest, they have a compensation. They now have a clear field ahead of them: reasonably clear, that is, of the colonial and neo-colonial heritage of structures, institutions and ruling attitudes. They can build, in the measure of their talent, from the "grass roots" of the society from which the leaders and militants of FRELIMO have themselves emerged.

Would you say they have now a better chance?

Yes, given that their liberation war was the only possible alternative to continued surrender or to defeat and death, I believe the compensation is a large one. It is not a compensation that came in any way automatically, let's insist on that again, but one that FRELIMO, and other movements like FRELIMO, have known how to extract and win from the miseries of war. Yes, and from the confusions of the time. It was my fortune to be the only European present at the second congress of FRELIMO, held in the bush of Niassa province in 1968. That was a crucial congress, once again illustrating the problem, for this was the congress which confirmed that FRELIMO would not compromise with the colonial system, but would fight on through to the end — the end that would give them this chance of building a new and democratic state from the "grass roots".

This was the congress, it seems to me, that will be seen as having enshrined FRELIMO's merit as a revolutionary movement. Their great merit — Cabral used to say this about all the liberation movements — was not to have fought for freedom and independence: that's always a duty, you can't expect praise for that. Their great merit was displayed at this second congress when, in that meeting in the woods of Niassa, threatened daily by Portuguese attack, an attack by colonial forces vastly superior in numbers and equipment, and at a comparatively early stage of the armed struggle, they showed that they could do much more than merely fight.

They proved, then and later, that they knew *how* to fight for freedom and independence in such a way that the wretchedness of war could be made to yield positive gains for the people of their country. And hasn't it been the same with every genuine movement of national liberation, in Africa or anywhere else? It is always better to avoid violence if you can, for violence is always destructive, even of the good that it may set itself to win: but there are times where you cannot avoid it. That's when you need wisdom. Any fool can use a gun, and fools can also have courage, but it takes great wisdom and a sense of collective responsibility, patient thought, and an enduring distrust of violence (above all, of your own violence) to use a gun to any purpose that can help society. That was what Samora* and his comrades of FRELIMO, above all in 1968 and after, showed that they possessed. They enabled their people — the broad masses of the people of Mozambique — to extract hope from despair, peace from war, understanding from confusion. They gave the rising generation, the men and women who will dominate the years ahead, a "starting chance" that was and that remains altogether more constructive, more rich in positive gains and possibilities, then any chance that ever existed before. This was their "compensation" for the violence of a war they had to fight; and yes, if you ask my opinion, it was and is a large one.

* Samora Maoisés Machel, military commander of FRELIMO's armed forces and president after the assassination of Eduards Mondlane by enemy agents in January 1969. President of Mozambique today.

IV

International Policy
and Local Conflicts

*You are a well known historian and an authority in the field of
African studies and many of your books – amongst them* Old
Africa Rediscovered, Black Mother *and* The Africans – *are rightly
said to be compulsory and enlightening reading for the Africans
themselves. You are also a much travelled witness of several
momentous events in Africa and have given us lively and moving
first hand accounts of the struggles in places like Guinea and
Angola. All this has endowed you with a unique insight into the
dynamics of Africa, past and present, so I would now like you to
take our discussion a stage further and place Africa in the wider
international context. What does foreign influence mean there
today?*

Emerging from direct colonial control, the new states of Africa
began their life in a "Western world" entirely dominated, if
indirectly, by the USA. Does this sound like an exaggeration?
Well, I remember being invited by a Nigerian university, early in
the 1960s, to open a new college of African studies. They would,
they explained, send me the necessary air ticket. But it turned
out that the new college was being funded by the University of
Michigan on finance given by the US Agency for International
Development; and this AID refused to pay for my ticket on the
grounds that my views were not sufficiently "respectable".
So the Nigerians were unable to send me an air ticket and had
to content themselves with someone else whose views *were*
sufficiently "respectable". It's what began to be called "neo-
colonialism": the initiative was Nigerian, but the actual choice
was not. A small detail, but perhaps an instructive one. Certainly,
in those days, it was indicative of the "general situation".

Now this American hegemony suited the British well enough,

and it also suited the French even if De Gaulle would have been the last to admit it. Gaullist policy in Africa could in fact operate only within the shelter of the American umbrella — the Anglo-American umbrella, if you prefer — which is no doubt why the chauvinism natural to Gaullism has found it so comforting to assert the contrary. A lot of Africans felt the same way. American hegemony continued to dominate the 1960s, but the '70s have brought a change. Analysis of the reasons why would take us too far afield. But the fact is beyond doubt. American hegemony is now under increasing challenge there. Because of Soviet activism in Africa? As a great power, the USSR naturally has its interest in whatever may occur in Africa. But the challenge to American hegemony — to "Western" hegemony in general — cannot be explained in terms of the familiar demonology of our so-called "national" but, really, insistently provincial media belonging to this or that capitalist group. It comes primarily from an African source. It marks another step towards those concepts of independence which seem, today, of major importance to African statesmen. It takes the form of "non-alignment". Much has been said about the ambiguities of "non-alignment". These certainly exist. Yet the thing itself is nevertheless real.

Take the example of Nigeria, again. At the end of 1975, the Americans were astonished to discover that they were unable to persuade a very "moderate" (not to say, very conservative) Nigerian military government to boycott and oppose the emergent Republic of Angola under the leadership of the MPLA.* They tried hard, as I happen to know from being in Lagos at the time, but they failed; and the Nigerians changed the whole diplomatic balance by carrying through their determination to recognise Angola. Why? Not from any sympathy with left-wing policies: on the contrary, the left-wing policies of the MPLA greatly bothered many Nigerians. But just because the Nigerians, above all those in control of the country at that time, were in revolt against that sort of indirect control of which I've given a very small personal example just now. They wanted — as they said privately — to "have a foreign policy of our own"; they were embarrassed at their relatively very powerful country continuing to appear as

*MPLA: People's Movement for Angolan Liberation, through whose struggle Angola became free of Portuguese colonial rule.

a docile instrument for whatever Washington and London might decide.

Now I think that this sentiment, qualify it how you will, joins together increasingly with a much more objective understanding of the *need* for non-alignment as a means of exercising independent choices in the matter of what may be good or not good for the Africans. Outside influences remain strong, sometimes they remain dominant (as in most of the little ex-French colonies); and the whole development of trans-national capitalism necessarily gives these outside influences a greater flexibility and strength. Yet the terms of the "contest" are changed. Whether in theory or practice, increasingly the "contest" becomes inter-African. And this "transposition", of course, is just one more way in which the history of Africa begins again after the colonial and neo-colonial interludes. It's true even in the francophone sphere. Whatever happens in the Ivory Coast may continue to depend upon Paris: all the same, along the West African seaboard in what used to be called Dahomey (and now is called, rather confusingly, Benin), the regime turns against its neo-colonialism and embarks on an attempt at structural change. That would have been very hard to imagine only a few years ago. It's not a simple trend, for all sorts of foreign influences are mixed up in certain aspects of non-alignment as well: all the same, it marks a trend — and a trend, in my opinion, that will grow in its importance.

In relation to foreign influences and indirect intervention, what about the American approach to African politics in general? How has it been developing and changing in the past few years? Can we talk of a different US attitude now? The crucial point of reference, the ultimate test, as we all know, remains South Africa, not so much in terms of its being the bastion of white supremacy (which has indeed become embarrassing at the diplomatic level vis à vis the other 'black' African states and world public opinion) but as the most powerful representative, in the final analysis, of what is the continuing economic interest of the West.

Up to the time of Nixon, American policy towards Africa was both consistent and intelligent from a capitalist point of view. Set going in its major premises by Roosevelt back in the days of the Atlantic Charter (1941) — the Charter of war aims, you'll remember, which promised under Rooseveltian insistence to allow all peoples, after the war, to choose the governments they wanted — this policy aimed at dismantling the African empires in such a way that their emergent parts entered and remained within the general politico-economic system dominated by Washington. And that is what this policy achieved, largely under Truman and Eisenhower. The British soon saw the wisdom of evacuating their political control in exchange for economic "continuity"; and even the French and Belgians, though kicking against it all the way, were eventually brought round to something of the same acceptance. By the time of the Eisenhower years, as we've seen, this policy had scored success practically all along the line — and American hegemony was such that even the names of visiting professors to African universities were going to be decided in Washington.

However limited, African political independence nonetheless had its reality. And part of this reality, after 1960, was that the Soviet Union and its partners now had at least a diplomatic access to Africa — an access soon enlarged by early forms of economic interchange. With the worst of the "Cold War" barely over and the hot war in Vietnam already on the way, this rattled the Americans; and their worry was again sharpened by events in the ex-Belgian Congo (Congo-Kinshasa, now Zaire) during 1960-61. Against American hostility to his programme and then to his person, Lumumba appealed to the Russians. The Russians could and did do little about this appeal, but the American reaction was very sharp. And with that we are into the Kennedy years and the rise of the CIA in Africa. American promotion of Mobutu dates from that moment; so, incidentally, does American promotion of the would-be Angolan "leader", Roberto Holden (of UPA, then FNLA). As far as we have learned from the admirable columns of the *Washington Post* and the *New York Times,* most of what the CIA did or attempted during the 1960s was of a stupidity that seems to be customary with "secret agencies" — who repeatedly employ the kind of persons, apparently, who see everything and understand nothing. But the important point is that the Americans now began to feel themselves on the defensive — precisely because their continued hegemony, which they had taken as something granted to them in permanence — was under threat.

That was the mark, in Africa, of the "Kennedy era". Johnson, after Kennedy, merely continued as before: I don't find anything in Johnson's policy that was different from Kennedy's except that Johnson persisted in manifest disaster (Vietnam) perhaps beyond the point where Kennedy might have drawn back. With Nixon there came indeed a difference. With him we are into the politics of gangsterdom. It is a remarkable "failure of nerve": and hence a failure of intelligence — in both senses, of information as well as of understanding. You see it in Kissinger's record in Africa. There the key document is the memorandum of the US National Security Council of 1970 — which considered the future of southern Africa. This arrived at the conclusion that the racist regimes in southern Africa would remain permanently in power, and that it must be wise American policy to support them. So Nixon continued to give the Portuguese dictatorship every possible aid in its wars against the national liberation movements in the Portuguese colonies: just as Johnson and indeed Kennedy had done before him. But the national liberation movements prevailed against the Portuguese dictatorship: indirectly, they even caused its overthrow. They also defeated Spínola's neo-colonialist plans of 1974, after the Lisbon coup d'etat. And that was when Kissinger, plunging from one kind of arrogance to another, compounded the misjudgement of the 1970 memorandum. With an astonishing naivety, defying even some of his best-informed officials, he put his money on the puppet Angolan "nationalists" of the FNLA and UNITA. Beyond that, he encouraged the South African regime to invade Angola. All this miserably failed, and at that point the US Congress, emerging from the disasters of Vietnam and Watergate, dug in its heels and cut off Kissinger's funds for subversion.

It was a very complete defeat. The Nigerian example again springs to mind. Suddenly it became clear that this great and powerful state, though governed by conservative generals, could not be relied upon to "do as it was told". Already Britain's ninth most important trading partner, already a major supplier of non-Arab oil to the USA, the Nigerians recognised the Republic of the MPLA. It was, as we said earlier, the clear evidence that the "balance of power and influence in Africa" was somehow changing — and not to American advantage: the proof, in my formulation, that Africans were once more beginning to make their own

history: a proof, in this respect, to be laid alongside the achievements of the various movements of national liberation. And since
then, of course, it's been Carter's concern, as I read it, to catch
up with and cancel out the blunders of his predecessors, especially
Nixon. And this, for me, has been the role of Ambassador Andrew
Young, no doubt a man whose political career may carry him far.

*What you said earlier on when we were reviewing this process of
change in Africa in connection with direct struggle is important.
You said that Angola represents a deciding point in the history
of the whole Continent, a climax, if I have understood you
correctly, in the catalogue of liberation wars in Africa . . .*

What I really meant was the failure of the enemies of the MPLA
to overturn it, the fact that the MPLA could succeed: this was the
deciding point.

*Yes, the success of the MPLA in Angola is significant in many
ways. Perhaps it is useful to recall once more here what repercussions the actual decolonisation process in the Portuguese
territories had on political events at home, from the overthrow
of the Salazar regime in April '74 to the fact that the politics of
liberation would eventually win Portuguese hearts and minds as
well. To quote from an essay of yours (*Southern Africa, The New
Politics of Revolution, *1976), "the political victory was larger
even than the military victory to which it had also given rise. This
political victory for the Africans was one that could become a
political victory for the Portuguese as well. History has not often
shown us anything like that". It's not as if the Angolan people
achieved their independence because it was perhaps easier to do
so in one of the most backward countries in Africa and because
they were fighting against a colonial enemy which was tired and
had lost its nerve. There was much more involved in this process
of liberation and its implications, as we can still see today, are
far wider.*

The reason why the liberation of Angola marks a deciding point
— I would compare it, regionally, with the liberation of Algeria
in North Africa more than ten years before — is precisely that it
could succeed against a massive array of international oppositions
and interventions. When the Algerians liberated their country, in

1962, they drove a deep wedge of independent thought and
action into the whole North African scene: the Angolans — with
their comrades in Mozambique — have driven a comparable wedge
into the southern African scene. On any longterm perspective,
and no matter how one may estimate the revolutionary claims of
Algeria or Angola, these have been decisive gains. They change
history. And it happens, of course, that Angola (like Algeria) is
potentially a very rich country: oil, diamonds, coffee, cotton,
iron, manganese, and so on. The multi-national corporations are
there, too: Gulf Oil, Krupp, De Beers, Tanganyika Concessions in
the case of Angola. But they don't control the situation. The
situation is controlled by the Angolans. If Gulf Oil should fail
to produce or deliver, the Angolans could very soon find a
substitute — and who could stop them? De Beers can control the
marketing of Angolan diamonds, but the Angolans control
the getting of them. The omnipotence of the trans-national
corporations becomes a myth wherever people are determined to
take their destiny in their own hands.

*Now the new Angola exposes South Africa even more vis à vis
the outside world for it emphasises the contradictions within
white society. South Africa, while perhaps becoming more vul-
nerable, is probably going to be more dangerous too. This is the
point from which one could re-examine the situation of South
Africa as its poses itself today.*

I agree, that's where the big test is going to come. The South
African racists have a weaker position today than ten years ago
— we can discuss the grounds for thinking so — and precisely for
this reason they become more dangerous, more apt to embark on
violent adventures. In this situation the problem for the Americans
and their partners is to know how to reduce or restrain racist
violence, but, at the same time, to know how to contain the
processes of change that are under way. The problem for the
Africans — and all those of us who see our road of progress as
passing *necessarily* by way of support for the Africans — is to
know how to promote these processes of change: precisely, to
prevent their being contained, tamed, reduced to neo-colonial
facades. It's a difficult problem either way, and no solutions "by
slogan and by dogma" are going to be of any use. All the same,
the problem now becomes *more* difficult for the racists than for

the Africans. For the latter, for us, it's a question of "helping history on its way". For the former, it's one of "holding up history" — of discovering how to continue to support racist rule while, at the same time, enjoying good commercial relations with a "black Africa" increasingly aware of its interests and responsibilities.

Reverting for a moment to your earlier question, about American policy, I'd say that with Carter we're back to the "general Rooseveltian line" — if I may put it in that otherwise misleading way: to a policy, that is, of intelligent and consistent promotion of capitalist interests in Africa within the limits — narrower than before — of their politico-economic options. They have evidently understood the point; as Ambassador Young has often explained. Others are slower to understand. The Federal German government appears the slowest of all, though with the government of President Giscard d'Estaing in close competition. They continue to think, it seems, that they can have their cake and eat it. They continue to enjoy the most privileged economic relations with racist South Africa while, at the same time, expecting "black Africa" to love them as brothers. The Germans are now finding out their mistake in Nigeria, where branches of German corporations which operate in South Africa are finding themselves under threat of expulsion. As for the French, the notion that their military intervention is going to bring them dividends is about as mistaken, as they will find, as their other notion that the opinions of Presidents Senghor and Houphouët-Boigny count in most of Africa for more than a row of pins. I put this a bit crudely: but after all this interview isn't an academic exercise. All these Franco-German "attitudes" belong to the past. They can still be operated and can still do a lot of damage, but essentially they're out-of-date. Again, South Africa is going to provide the acid test. For us in Britain, perhaps, above all.

The faith of the Americans in the concrete capability of South Africa to stand up economically for itself and to be able to defend itself militarily may not be greatly diminished but, as you have just said, it's going to be more and more difficult for them to have good normal relations with black Africa. This is why perhaps they feel obliged to have some of their spokesmen from time to time talk about the desirability of change in Southern

Africa, within the white racist societies there. They are measuring up to the need of at least being seen to be favouring change. What do you think of this?

I think that one doesn't need to suppose it to be insincere. The Americans are not stupid and they have understood that progressive change in South Africa is very much what is required, whether from a commercial or moral point of view. The fact remains that until very recently, indeed until Carter became president, there was absolutely no sign at all of any American pressure on South Africa. There have been one or two signs since then. There are those who say that the economic situation in South Africa, relying as it does quite largely upon the external gold price, had become difficult: because, they say, American influence, whether exercised through the World Bank or otherwise, had deliberately depressed the price of gold. It has risen again now, but it was depressed. And it seems to me that there are real if uneasy attempts by the Americans at this stage to oblige the South African regime to liberalise − that is, to the point where that regime may become able to *contain* the processes of protest and challenge which are now coming ever more strongly from the African masses.

Let's carry the debate a little further. The Americans, and they are not alone in this respect, the British also, would very much like to liberalise the situation in South Africa. But the South African regime continues to apply the full rigour of its apartheid policy in every field of life. The difficulty for the South African regime in liberalising is in itself extremely great. You only have to consider that they have divided South Africa into two zones, the so-called black homelands, and the so-called white areas. Now in the black homelands, which are about 12% of South Africa's territory, there is a population at the moment of about seven million people. Seven million people with no industry, no advanced form of economy at all, living not even in villages but more or less like a labour reserve available for use in the white areas. But in the white areas, permanently in the white areas, there are eight million Africans, and these eight million Africans are indispensable to the South African economy; nothing can be done without them. To dismantle the apartheid system it would be necessary to give these eight million Africans all the civil rights which they now don't have, it would be necessary to make them citizens, to give them voting rights, to lift off all the pass restrictions. But for the white South Africans to do that it would be necessary for them to go through a revolutionary change of mind. All one can say at the moment is that there is absolutely no sign at all of this revolutionary change of mind — only a few cosmetic "changes".

On the contrary, what we have at present is a doubling and redoubling of the South African military expenditure, so that South Africa today, in terms of hitting power, is immensely stronger than any other state in Africa. That's to say it has got, and there again largely thanks to the Germans and the French, a very advanced missile capacity. It may even be about to make a nuclear bomb. And of course this reinforces the white racist regime in the feeling that it can survive, even against the pressures of the US, or anybody else. It can defeat any internal uprising, and it can prevent any intervention by other African states, it can smash any other Africa state that likes to go against them. So they think.

On the other hand it's impossible not to notice, in this matter of military strength, that it conceals a major weakness, and this is the weakness of manpower. There are in South Africa today four or five million whites against some twenty million non-whites. The only persons admitted into the armed services, the only persons allowed to carry arms, are the whites. This means that this enormous armoury which they have built up, this over-whelming armoury, is terribly short of manpower. It's fit for a blitzkrieg, a rapid strike, but it cannot carry on a war for very long because it hasn't got the manpower. If you imagine a situation in which the South Africans suddenly embark upon a kind of war of destruction against this or that African state, whether it be Angola, Zambia or Mozambique, and imagine the reaction of that on the rest of black Africa, and if you then consider the major interests which the Western powers have in the rest of Africa, you'll see that with every increase of South Africa's military threat, there is a greater fear in the West that this threat may be carried out. The big question still remains open, though: what is the West going to do about this threat?

Out of this comes certainly a confused reply, but one aspect of that reply seems to me to be that as things are going now there is going to be an increasing isolation of the white regime. It doesn't guarantee that there will not be a war. We may be moving to most dramatic situations, we may be moving in Southern Africa into another big international conflict. But it does mean that if that conflict doesn't happen, the white regime becomes more and more isolated as the economic, political, and diplomatic weight of the rest of Africa is more and more unitedly against that regime. So I would see across the next years (I emphasise that it will not be tomorrow morning) an increasing isolation of the white regime, an increasing demand by all African states that that isolation should be increased by the deliberate action of all those external partners of South Africa. We now even have a possibility of economic sanctions against South Africa. When that idea was first mooted some ten years ago it seemed utopian, it was laughed out of court, it was said "this will never happen". Now we see that it could happen. In the case of Britain the economic interests in the rest of Africa are far greater today than they are in South Africa even if Britain remains the biggest investor in South Africa. The same has become true of the US.

Yet we know that the degree of economic integration of the West has increased tremendously and that South Africa is an integral and in many ways essential part of the western system. Some underline too the strategic importance of this connection. Much as outside pressures of various kind might be exercised to bring about some form of change in South Africa, the West would probably never do anything in practice to substantially damage the South African economy or to imperil that basic link. There are therefore conflicting tendencies at work between fostering change on one hand and wanting to preserve the common fundamental economic interests. Isn't there a contradiction?

I wouldn't put it on a moral basis at all. I merely think that change is under way and that the interests of foreign investors in South Africa are to act in such a way that they can have their cake and eat it, that they can contain these processes of change. But the problem is, can they?

What do you think is the time scale on that?

Oh a fairly long one. One shouldn't have the illusion that the South African system is anywhere near the point of collapse. One shouldn't have the illusion that forces of African resistance are near the point where they can become effective in imposing change. One has to see it once again from the standpoint of historical process. What's happening is that in relative terms the South African system today is weaker than it was, say, ten years ago — let alone twenty years ago. It is weaker for two reasons. First because the interest of its foreign supporters in the rest of Africa are greater than they were before. You only have to think of oil: if South Africa were an oil producing country that might be a different matter, but they have not been able to find any oil at all while Nigeria and Angola have become major suppliers of oil to the Western world. Secondly, the forces of African resistance, though still relatively weak and disorganised, are stronger than they were ten or twenty years ago. This is a process of change, a long process. I wouldn't put a term of years on it, but we are concerned in these last decades of the twentieth century with a trend of change which is probably irresistible.

It's in this perspective that we come back to your question: isn't there a contradiction? Yes, inherently it was always there — in practice, though, it's become apparent to the makers of Western policy only in the last three years or so, maybe less. Or rather, what's become apparent is that the contradiction has become so sharp as to cause Western policy-makers to want to *do something* about resolving it. Given the changing balance — whether inside Africa or globally — the most intelligent of these policy-makers now see the problem as being one of pushing the South African regime into a process of "internal decolonisation": but in such a way, of course, that this doesn't risk the substance of capitalist interests. By which I mean the continued enclosure of the South African system within the general Western system.

That is difficult, of course, and mostly because of the stubborn and intransigent nature of the South African regime: a fully indigenous racism now in control of an indigenous capitalism, even if that capitalism remains dependent on the general system. But it is necessary, all the same: for without some movement towards liberalising change in South Africa there are no "safety valves", and so, always, the risk of more huge explosions like Soweto in 1976, and more bloody repressions. Besides that, the evidence shows that internal African protest is now acquiring new and effective forms of political organisation: as yet, of course, often underground. All this being so, and with its international implications, the West will find that it must push harder for concessions. It must even, possibly, entertain the threat of economic sanctions: at least, of a deliberate process of dis-investment by Western corporations. What seemed "unrealistic" only yesterday wears a different look today; another trend that will continue.

The Namibian case is characteristic. For decades, the Western powers prevented any effective action, through the UN or how-ever, to undermine the South African colonial hold on Namibia. They simply put a wall of defence around that South African colony. All those of us who pressed for a policy of liberating Namibia were treated as simpletons or knaves. Now it's different. Now the Western Powers — even Federal Germany and France, however hard that is to imagine — are actively trying to bring about a "solution" in Namibia which be tantamount to an "internal decolonisation". Now it's the simpletons or knaves, it seems, who were right all along — up to a point, of course! For the Western powers make their attempt, naturally, within the limits of a neo-colonial model. That's their way of trying to resolve the contradiction you mentioned. Can they pull it off? Not in the short run, as it now seems, for the South African racists look like getting away with their "internal solution" in Namibia. But that's no kind of solution for the long run. Here too the Africans will win, even if racist manoeuvres are going to raise still higher the price they must pay.

One of the ways in which South Africa was thinking of protecting itself was to promote and strengthen a buffer zone to the North against black Africa with satellites or puppet states providing a kind of cordon sanitaire. In the last few years however the Portuguese colonies have collapsed and change in Rhodesia has become increasingly likely. How do you see the problems faced by Rhodesian whites vis à vis the guerilla war in their country and consequently the problem that this poses for South Africa itself?

It's an extension of the same argument, isn't it? The Rhodesian case, the Zimbabwean case, is another piece of evidence relating to the weakness of racist South Africa today, relative to its position of ten years ago or little more. In 1965, with South African encouragement, the white minority in Rhodesia (about

quarter of a million to about six million blacks), rebelled against
the British Crown and declared their "unilateral independence".
They got away with it to begin with because there were interests
in Britain powerful enough to prevent any effective action against
that rebellion: there was no British military response, and the
critically important oil sanction was never applied with the
necessary vigour. After that the Rhodesian racists continued
to get away with it because they had the full and multilateral
support of South Africa — diplomatically, commercially, finan-
cially, and of course psychologically. As you say, the South
African racists thought that their dependents in Rhodesia would
serve as a useful buffer between South Africa and black nationalism in the rest of Africa.

It didn't work. In 1975 the other two great buffers, Angola
and Mozambique, collapsed. Liberated, those countries became
militant supporters of African liberation and the whole balance
changed. There was suddenly the dire possibility, even then a
probability, that Rhodesia would now become transformed
into a militant Zimbabwe governed by a party comparable with
FRELIMO in Mozambique or MPLA in Angola. And so we had,
in due course, the American attempt, which proved successful, to
pressure the South African and then the Rhodesian governments
into accepting majority rule in Rhodesia. The whites there had
sworn blue in the face that they would never accept majority
rule, not within a hundred years: now they had to accept it
within two years. As a means, once again of outflanking the radical
trends in Zimbabwean nationalism: as a means of containing
African pressures which could no longer be merely suppressed.

Will this plan work? We don't know. On one side the sheer
intransigence of the Rhodesian whites, epitomised by Ian Smith,
has worked usefully for the radical elements in Zimbabwean
nationalism. This intransigence has made it easy for them to
show that compromise with the whites must mean defeat for the
blacks. On the other side, the internal divisions in Zimbabwean
nationalism — and above all within the radical groups of the
Patriotic Front — have repeatedly weakened the chance for a
FRELIMO-type solution — a solution, that is, which can produce
a genuine independence. The armed struggle of the fighters of the
Patriotic Front has gone far to dominate the whole country, and
grows week by week in strength. Yet the whites have been able to

find many African partners, and the divisions within the Patriotic Front have helped them to find more. Talking as we are before the outcome is in any way clear, we can perhaps reach two conclusions. One is that the cause of African liberation from racist rule has scored a way or success in Zimbabwe. The other is that this success still remains to be confirmed.

To see what the Africans themselves have been able to do about all these problems, can we look at the history of the Organisation of African Unity (OAU) itself?

The Organisation of African Unity was founded in 1963 on a very ambitious charter of all-African continental unity providing for all-African executives, defence staff etc. None of that has been realised, or could have been realised (any more than the UN has been able to become a "world government") and the OAU has been much criticised for becoming little more than a talking shop. There is a good deal of truth in that, but again it is unrealistic to see only this aspect of it. The OAU in fact was one of the principal gains scored by the first period of decolonisation. It is an organisation that has enabled the African governments to come together and discuss their problems and to present, as it were, a common front against a world which was still on the whole ignorant of and often hostile towards Africa. It enabled them to organise their forces more easily at the UN and it enabled them to solve, temporarily at least, a number of frontier disputes. It enabled an all-African diplomacy to evolve and the formation of an all-African development bank. It also helped the Africans to see themselves in relation to the rest of the world. The OAU has been, in short, a useful intrument.

So you wouldn't draw a completely negative balance sheet for this organisation that our mass media often like to present in a bad light . . .

On the contrary. That is another piece of provincial vulgarity to which our mass media (at any rate in Britain) is constantly subject. Our media often show towards Africa an attitude of ignorance and mythological prejudice which would be entirely comical in its pretentions if it didn't reflect so badly on the culture of our country. The OAU has been a useful instrument but it has limits. It is no more capable of solving the problems of Africa than the UN can solve those of the world. It is a forum of governments, of presidents, a meeting place for "top persons": useful to some extent, useless beyond that. And if you look at the whole question of frontiers which you raised and we were talking about earlier, you see the positive and negative side of the OAU very clearly indeed. In 1964, meeting in Cairo, the OAU confronted this question of frontiers. Everybody knew the frontiers were irrational, had been drawn by the colonial powers; but on the other hand it was said, very realistically, that if you started to alter one lot of frontiers, then there would be no end to it. So we must lay down a rule, they said, that the colonial frontiers are going to be accepted. And they were right.

That's a defensive attitude, trying to consolidate the existing situation and avoiding more trouble because one knows how dangerous it could be . . .

Well, dangerous and not dangerous. If you look at what's happened, there have been surprisingly few frontier disputes. Generally speaking, most African peoples have accepted the frontiers within which they have become established, and the action of the OAU has tended to diminish the dangers of conflicts in the meantime. At this meeting in 1964, let's recall, the OAU passed a resolution designed to settle the question of frontiers in Africa, or, at least, to put that question on ice for as long as that might be. We must all, the OAU governments agreed, accept the colonial frontiers we have inherited, and we must not seek to change them. For if one or two governments should try to change them, and should succeed, then there might be no end to the frontier disputes which would result from that.

Generally, of course, this was a wise decision: another proof of the capacities of African statesmanship when it is exercised. But it had a weakness. Its weakness was that it allowed for no exceptions, above all not for the most obvious exception of all: that of the frontiers of imperial Ethiopia. For the Ethiopia of 1964 was not, and had never been, a colony, except for a six-year fascist occupation between 1935 and 1941. On the contrary, it was a sovereign state whose *imperial* frontiers were drawn during the great colonial "share-out" of the last decades of the

19th century — that's to say it was the Empire of Menelik. Consequently, it had always had — and it certainly had in 1964 — a very acute "national question", above all in respect of the Solami region of the Ogaden, and of Eritrea.

Let's recall that before Somalia became independent, and was still ruled by Italian trusteeship, the Emperor of Ethiopia had been manoeuvring to bring the *whole* of Somalia inside Ethiopia. In fact the Somali delegation at the OAU meeting of 1964, the meeting which tried to sweep all frontier questions under the carpet, refused to sign the resolution in question. They walked out of the conference at that point. We have been claiming the Ogaden, they argued, ever since the 1880s. We continue to claim it now. Our dispute with the Ethiopian empire is more than 70 years older than your resolution; and you cannot simply ask us to suppress our claim. They were at the same time in dissidence with Kenya, again over a Somali region long since included in Kenya. That's part of history and cannot be wiped out, and if you are going to form a general rule and not take account of such exceptions as these, then clearly you are going to run into trouble. It goes without saying, I think, that peace and progress in the whole region of the Horn of Africa cannot be achieved in any stable manner until the "national question" inside the existing Ethiopian territorial structure (identical, territorially, with an imperial structure) is settled by major concessions to self-determination: above all in respect of the Somali Ogaden and Eritrea.

But if that is obvious, it is just as obviously difficult — and rendered much more difficult by a whole series of deplorable foreign actions. I mention the example of the Horn only to suggest that any consistent programme for "moving beyond nationalism" in Africa is, undoubtedly, one for the future: even possibly a remote future. Yet my own opinion, for what it may be worth, is that this problem of "moving beyond nationalism" is one that will become mature, demanding at least the beginnings of a solution, a good deal sooner than may appear from the superficial evidence today. And this is what the situation in the Horn also appears to indicate.

To begin with, one may note that the idea of permanently congealed frontiers — the permanent acceptance of the colonial frontiers, that is — is a very new one. The best and greatest pioneers of "classical decolonisation" in the 1950s — the men whose ideas led the way in breaching the colonial bastions — were all of the opinion that an independent Africa should move rapidly, even at once, towards a reorganisation of nation-state units into large regional federations or confederations. Nkrumah and Sékou Touré thought that; and they even proclaimed, as a nominal gesture to the need for such a frontier reorganisation, a "union" between Ghana and Guinea. The best leaders of the Rassemblement Démocratique Africain in West and Equatorial French Africa — that RDA which carried the banners of African resurgence into the constituent assemblies of the Fourth French Republic in 1946 — were all of the view that the twelve colonial territories should be reorganised, after independence, into two large confederations. Nyerere stood for the same idea in the three colonies of British East Africa. There was even a proposal to unify the Maghreb — and so on.

These unifying ideas failed because they were destroyed by the "neo-colonial" mode of decolonisation. Once in power, the ruling groups in these emergent countries, or most of them, saw their interest in retaining a strictly separate identity: to the point, as we have seen, that by 1964 there was no more talk of any kind, in the OAU or anywhere else, of moving toward regional unities. Formed as an instrument of unifying Africa, in certain basic ways the OAU has been obliged to function as an instrument that guarantees *disunity*. I am not saying, of course, that this trend was avoidable. I doubt very much if it was avoidable. It may have been inevitable, in so far as anything in history is inevitable. I am only saying that the *acceptance* of a permanently disunited Africa — divided into some fifty nation-states — is a product of these "neo-colonialist" years; was never part of the progressive heritage of African nationalism in the past; and comes, now, more and more against its own frustration.

This is a wide and useful picture of one of the most acute issues now under discussion and of the general background from which it moves. You have outlined the problems of the Southern regions of Africa and now those of the Horn. In both these areas the situation remains serious and might become even worse. What do you think is going to happen?

If the Western bloc persists in supporting the South African
racists against all those pressures making for a democratic revolution in South Africa, then there obviously arises a corresponding
danger for the non-aligned states of Africa — the most important
states, as it happens — that these will be shoved off their ground
of non-alignment by the sheer dynamics of international policy.
Or if the French continue with their policy of maintaining client
states, or trying to build new ones, *manu militari,* then again
they tend to push an independent Africa from a position of non-
alignment to one of hostility. Or it can be argued — as I would
argue — that the action of the Soviet bloc in actively supporting
the persistence of the Ethiopian imperial frontiers — imperial
frontiers, let us remember, acquired during and after the European
share-out — against the demands of leading nationalities for self-
determination (Somalis and Eritreans), is another example of
active infringement of African independence. Of course, circumstances alter cases. Soviet support for the MPLA in Angola,
beyond any doubt, was a very positive contribution to African
non-alignment, to African independence.
positive contribution to African non-alignment, to African
independence.

*How do the Africans feel about this ever-present framework of
East-West confrontation which impinges upon events in Africa
and is an ever-present influence?*

If you leave out South Africa, an issue with fearful potentials for
disaster, then there seems at present little likelihood of any
direct Great-Power confrontation in Africa. That's, partly,
another product of African independence: no small one, either.
The confrontation is indirect: a competitive searching for positions
of influence. It sways back and forth. It repeatedly tests the two
Super-Powers not only in their capacity to deliver material aid to
their chosen friends, but more and even much more in their
intentions, in the inner nature of their policies, in the depth of
their understanding. It's a contest that Africans tend to watch
with a range of emotions that goes from sheer astonishment to
considerable fear: but, with a growing sophistication of judgement
and experience, they also find this contest very educative. In the
case of Angola, for instance, they saw the USA doing all those

things which combined to a result most pleasing to the USSR. In the case of the Horn of Africa, on the contrary, they see the USSR abandoning a left-wing Somalia; aiding the Ethiopians in an effort to wipe out the ELPF in Eritrea, a left-wing and there-fore genuine movement of liberation; and, in Ethiopia itself, backing a military dictatorship which, as many suspect, can still go "either way". They see the USSR, in short, doing all those things which combine to a result most pleasing to the USA. All this, indeed, is so comforting to the right that here in Britain even *The Times* has been writing in glowing terms of the EPLF — something you couldn't easily have imagined a year or so back. So it's a Super-Power contest, waged indirectly, that will sway back and forth. Its major effect, I think, it always to reinforce for Africans the attractiveness of policies of non-alignment.

What about the Cubans?

To their lasting credit, the Cubans have been giving revolutionary aid to Africa for a long time: ever since 1966, when Guevara was active there. They were a valuable and much valued source of fraternal aid for all the liberation movements in the Portuguese colonies — and pretty well from the outset of those liberation wars. They made room in their schools for African children from the liberated zones, they sent their doctors into those zones, they provided training facilities for fighters, they did all they could. And they crowned all that with the courage and generosity — and self-sacrifice — of their aid to Angola in the moment of its greatest peril. They went to Angola with enormous difficulty. They had no long-range aircraft. They had no big ships. But they got there, and as soon as they got there they went into action against the South African and Zairean invaders: with the good results we know. Their response to the MPLA's call for their aid — and it certainly wasn't any Soviet pressure that took them to Angola — makes one of the really great moments in modern African history. And the Cubans stay in Angola now, again at MPLA's request, so as to guarantee the security of that young republic until its own armed forces are strong enough to take over the job. More than that, they give Angola a lot of useful aid in the non-military field. When I was last in Angola, mid-1977, there were no fewer than 300 Cuban doctors working there: in a country which had been obliged to begin its independent life, late in 1975, with no more than a dozen doctors for the whole population. The Cuban record in Angola, let's insist on that, has proved admirable and positive.

And in the Horn? A different thing. If you deplore Soviet policy in the Horn, as I do, then you're bound to deplore Cuban policy as well. It's a policy, in any case, that is hard to understand. Its only justification, so far as I can see, is on the argument that the success of the Ethiopian revolution has depended and will continue to depend upon maintaining the Ethiopian imperial frontiers — and even, within those, much of the substance of the Ethiopian imperial structure. But that is a contradiction in terms, because it involves a refusal to solve the national question, inside those frontiers, in the only way in which it can be solved now — that is, by far-reaching policies of self-determination for at least the major minority nationalities. My own view, for what's it worth, is that the Cubans in this case failed to study Ethiopian history. Fidel's original idea, incontestably the right one, was to work towards a progressive confederation of states in the Horn. And this might have worked very well if only the regime in Addis had been willing — and *able,* given its relative weakness and immaturity — to accept it. But that regime would only accept it upon condition that the national minorities inside Ethiopia continued to accept the domination of Addis Ababa. That was Soviet policy, of course, and it then became Cuban policy. A great pity, at least. The right policy — if it won't sound pretentious in me for saying it — was to guarantee the security of the military regime in Addis, and all the revolutionary changes which had followed the overthrow of the emperor in 1974, notably the anti-feudal land reforms: while, at the same time, working for self-determination in the Ogaden and in Eritrea. After which the situation of other large nationalities, notably the Oramo, could have been tackled in an appropriate manner. Out of that you really might have got a confederation of progressive states. As it is, you have got nothing of the kind, and there may be worse to follow. Or so it seems to me.

American spokesmen have repeatedly accused the Cubans of exercising a destablising influence in the politics of Africa and this kind of accusation has recently been levelled against them in the strange and tragic episode of the Shaba province of the Congo.

I believe that belongs to the realm of cold-war propaganda. The Cubans have not acted as in any way an element of destabilisation. In Angola they acted as an element of stability. Even Ambassador Young has told us that. In Ethiopia they have also acted as an element of stability, in the sense that they have tried to uphold the integrity of the Ethiopian imperial geographical structure: to my mind regrettably, but there it is. In Shaba they simply have not acted at all. There was no evidence of any Cuban intervention in Shaba in 1977, and there was none in 1978. The Cubans themselves have denied any such intervention, but one doesn't even have to rely upon their word, it simply has not occurred. And may I note that if it *had* occurred, then Mr Mobutu's situation in Shaba would have ceased to exist.

What do you make of the recent French initiative and their renewed and extraordinary interest in African politics? On the other hand, what do you think of the contacts between Zaire and Angola?

A very clear demonstration, once again, of the destructive effects of the kind of policies advocated by President Giscard d'Estaing. If French proposals for a kind of "fire brigade", ready at any moment to fly off into Africa in defence of this or that specific European or American interest, had been realised, then Mobutu in Zaire would no doubt still be on his years-old ground of outright hostility to Angola – he'd continue to maintain, between Zaire and Angola, a frontier of war. Fortunately, these proposals were not followed: the British wouldn't have them, and then the Americans (who had tried hard but failed to find "another Mobutu") decided that the British were right. So the Americans put the screws on Mobutu, and Mobutu has had to sing another tune. He had to come to an amicable agreement with the government of Angola. A frontier of war becomes — let's hope it stays like that — a frontier of peace. A real success, in other words for a policy of constructive détente and non-alignment. In personal terms, — though he'd never have used them — this was a success for President Agostinho Neto.

At the end of this exhaustive review of places, peoples, problems and tensions which are very much under scrutiny now and which pose quite a few question marks upon the future of Africa, let us go back to what you were saying earlier about African nationalism, its limitations and contradictions. How, then, can Africans get themselves beyond this point, beyond the constrictions of the structures within which they have to operate? How can they overcome this bourgeois nation-state nationalism, which you have so lucidly illustrated through history to the present day, and which they were obliged to accept in order to become independent? It is this very nationalism which now threatens to stultify all further progress isn't it?

Well, I think myself that its the same question as before: how can they get themselves beyond the "neo-colonial" model? I shall not be so pretentious as to suggest that I know the answer. Who does know the answer — outside the verbalism of theoretical abstraction? But I am no less sure that the history of these coming years will provide, will have to provide, the answer.

For the alternative is not pleasant to contemplate. The alternative is an Africa permanently divided into a host of nation-states of which a majority are far too small, or territorially ill-structured, to be able to develop from their own resources: an Africa, that is, permanently in prey to foreign domination in one form or another. And here, perhaps, one finds the strongest argument in favour of the radical regimes now beginning to appear and develop in various parts of Africa. They may or may not be able to solve this continental "national question". But only they, as matters stand today, appear to possess the potentials of being able to solve it.

V

Towards a New Africa

In our conversation we have come a long way through the history, culture and past and present policies in Africa and you have been able to talk about it with the knowledge and authority which come from a 30-year association with your subject and field of interests. At this point I would like to simply ask you, what do you wish for Africa in the future?

Well, without entering on banalities such as that one wishes for peace, happiness and progress, I suppose that what one wishes most is that Africa will be able, with as little pain as may be, to complete "the revolution of independence". To find its way out of the constrictions of nationalism. To unite its energies and resources so as to build truly egalitarian economies of development. Yes, and to give full scope to the enlargement and enrichment of its manifold cultures. In this discussion we've had to leave out so much; we've necessarily had to stick to the hard and gritty issues that claim everyday attention. They can give a lop-sided picture. They can also be boring. But Africa isn't boring, isn't ever boring. In thirty years I've never found it so. On the contrary, the last thirty years have brought a marvellous resurgence in every field of culture. Poets, novelists, dramatists, cineasts, sculptors, painters – all these have found a place for themselves and their work such as never existed before. A place, besides, which is increasingly their own – and less and less a place occupied as some kind of "reflection" of this or that external fashion or set of criteria. That's another good trend that will continue, another gain of the last thirty years.

Another thing I've learned is not to worry too much. Maybe we worry too much in Europe. The Africans certainly have a mass of troubles on their hands, but the "general tone" isn't one of worry and depression. It's a remarkably resilient capacity for pushing along with their lives. Laughter — they laugh a lot in Africa. Europeans — well, my Scottish Presbyterian ancestors, my Great-Aunt Jeannie, all that solemn tribe, they'd find that very wrong: you've troubles, you shouldn't laugh, it's serious. Yes, it's serious. But it's comical as well. Who in their right mind didn't laugh at the buffooneries of the dreadful Bokassa, Great Leader, Supreme Commander-in-Chief, Lord of the Prancing Lion, and king of kings of the Central African Empire — where there's more poverty per square kilometre than in almost any other country in the continent? Who didn't laugh at the antics of the horrific Field-Marshal Idi Amin Dada (with an army totalling three battalions, or was it four?), especially when he tweaked the nose of arrogant Europeans?* Who takes all these pretentious charlatans seriously — except themselves? If you didn't laugh at the spectacle, you'd have to cry; and Africans, on the whole, prefer to laugh. I do too.

I don't find myself worried about the future of Africa. I don't know if Africans are going to be able to solve their problems any better (or worse) than the rest of us. What's important for all of us, in our time, is that Africans *have the chance* to solve their own problems. That we rid the world of this whole incubus of racism, of colonial fascism under any guise. That we clear the ground. After that, things will go better. I'm sometimes accused of being an "optimist": by persons, of course, who think things will go worse. That doesn't worry me either. It's too bad for them. Those who know Africa from the inside, or at least have tried to know Africa from the inside, see things differently. They know that the potential situation in Africa today, with all the problems that exist and are even getting more severe, is nonetheless relatively far better, far more hopeful, than it was thirty years ago.

You come back to what we were saying earlier: about the age of the continent's population. Half of it is under twenty, another large segment between twenty and thirty. These young men and women are entering a realm of opportunities which didn't exist before — a realm of possible freedom, of possible development, of possible enjoyment of life, that was barely thinkable as long as the colonial systems and their racist cultures maintained their suffocating grip. I don't find any ground for pessimism in that.

*Written before the happy overthrow of this sanguinary dictator in May 1979.

You have gone through a lot of experiences yourself in the African continent. You have seen very important moments of history in the making, have shared hopes and labours and sufferings with liberation movements in action, and you have witnessed some dramatic moments at close quarters. What episodes do you remember most from your rich and — may I add — still continuing African diary?

I've just been reading Amendola's *Una Scelta di Vita,** a beautiful book. What came out of it, for me, was above all the richness of the friendships that were given to him, even in the hardest times. My own measure of trials and tribulations have been insignificant, perfectly minimal, when compared to his: all the same, *mutatis mutandis,* it's been the same for me. I've had the great good fortune, I have it still, to have been given many friendships. They are what I remember. At all the levels you can think of. Not a bit dramatic, for the most part. Journeys of discovering history: journeys of discovering people — in Africa at any rate, outside the archives, it's been the same thing. Driving up through the forests of Asante to the fields of Kintampo, with the morning mist on the trees, and finding my friend Hajj Osmanu under a black umbrella in a field of maize inspecting his crop, and going on with him to Wa, and sitting with the elders of that venerable city under their "assembly tree" — for you need shade in Wa — and listening to their wisdom of the ancestors. Arriving in Darfur, far out in the savannahs of the Eastern Sudan, and finding the friendship of a local governor who lends me a truck, and we go in that truck through the hills north of Jebel Marra, the great mountain standing like a lost ship in the desert, to inspect the ruins of Uri and Ain Farah. Living in the bush with comrades of the liberation movements, seeing them make history. Enjoying friendships that nothing can destroy, not even time. Knowing oneself trusted, needed, relied upon. I sit here now in my old English city and I think of all those friendships, and I feel singularly blessed.

Not long ago, a year or so, one of Vorster's political prisoners was released from Pretoria jail at the end of a long sentence. A fine man, not in the least broken by the degradations of that bitter experience, but also a man well marked by Vorster's police:

---

*A Choice of Life. Georgio Amendola is one of Italy's veteran heroes of the fight against fascism and for democratic revolution.

and so he made his way — oh, in this way and in that — to England. He sought me out, and said to me: That book of yours, the one about the liberation of Guinea-Bissau — it was very useful to us, it brought us great encouragement. I asked him: But how could you read it in Pretoria jail? The answer was that some friend had smuggled it into the "politicals" and they'd passed it from hand to hand, hiding it from the warders. That was another moving moment for me, the kind that makes you feel your life worthwhile.

On the other side — yes, losses too: fearful losses. One doesn't forget those. Losses that dig a gulf into your life that nothing can fill. Medhi Ben Barka, Félix Moumié (I never had the opportunity to know his greater comrade, Reuben Um Nyobé), Eduardo Mondlane, Saidi Mingas, so many others whose lives were taken long before their time. And Amílcar Cabral, struck down by the agents of fascism in 1973, among the greatest and the best of the human beings of our time. He'd come to me in London in 1960, and we worked together and we were friends. Our families became each other's families. Late in 1972 I was on one of my trips in the liberated zones of Guinea-Bissau: we said farewell over supper in his house as Christmas lay ahead. And then, a few weeks later, the telephone rang in my London house. The BBC. This murder, they said, this murder of Cabral, please comment now — I didn't believe them, but I had to believe them. The anger and the sorrow remain. Not only, though. The joy too, even a vivid joy to illuminate the loss, that such a man existed, worked to such great effect, changed the realities of our world. That one could be with him on his route.

I think Cabral was particularly important because he was a man who was able to express himself in a very articulate way. He was quite at ease with theory and capable of thinking very deeply about the long term course of events in Africa. His loss may be felt all the more because it was a loss (although a temporary one) for political theory on the African Continent, for the theory of the 'African Revolution'. We may well have passed beyond the age of the charismatic style of leaders like Nkrumah, but we shall certainly never go beyond the need for power of analysis, foresight and theory. Perhaps it is at this stage along the path to a 'new Africa', that those precious qualities are particularly in demand.

We shall never get beyond the phase when the best people are needed. And you make a good concluding point. The charismatic heroes, the great tribunes of the people, the word-spinners, the "populists" — and what a range of extraordinary men and women they have been, running the whole gamut of human nature — they played their part in those years of "early decolonisation". They helped to batter down the doors of the colonial systems — sometimes having a vague notion of where they were going, very often having none. Then it was another kind of struggle from today, a more limited and in some ways much easier struggle: to get rid of the structures and cultures of "imposed inferiority", of inbuilt and ingrained discrimination, of direct colonial racism.

Today it's a different struggle. In the senses we've been talking about, it's to build a new society, egalitarian, democratic, increasingly capable of realising and uniting — realising because uniting — the potentials of Africa's peoples, the potentials that could not be and cannot be realised within the institutional confines and the cultural assumptions taken over from Africa's former masters. Today it's entirely necessary for Africa's leaders, at the top but also down the ranks, to know where they are going, and why they are going there, and how they are going to get there. And the best of those leaders — they're not so few, either — know this far better than anyone outside Africa. That's another reason for optimism. A good reason, too.

Spokesman Title

The Kissinger Study of Southern Africa

When Dr. Henry Kissinger comissioned this secret study of
U.S. policy options in southern Africa, he little thought
that it would become a public document. It stands alongside *The Pentagon Papers* and the secret documents of the
International Telephone and Telegraph Corporation on
Chile in its importance as a source of public understanding
of how political decisions are made in Washington.

Southern Africa poses a crucial question for U.S. policy
makers. What attitude should they take to the white racist
power base and to apartheid? How should they respond to
the pressures of black African states? What are U.S. strategic,
military, economic and other interests in the area? What
should the U.S. say at the U.N.? What about the black liberation movements? What are the roles of the Soviet Union
and China?

All these policy questions and many more are summarised
in these pages, and the alternatives for the U.S. are set out.
The reader is afforded a unique opportunity to see the
mind of official Washington at work.

Cloth £3.00   *Paper £1.25*

Class and Revolution in Ethiopia

by John Markakis and Nega Ayele

A fascinating and detailed account of the dramatic events
in Ethiopia during the three years up to mid-1977. It por-
trays the forces that generated the revolution of 1974,
details the overthrow of Haile Selassie's regime and documents the subsequent development of the new military
regime which led it to turn on the popular movement
that brought it into being.

Nega Ayele was murdered in one of the purges of the
left in 1977. John Markakis, a scholar who has written
extensively on Ethiopia, has now completed the work
they began together.

Cloth £6.00   *Paper £2.50*

Enquiries   to   Bertrand   Russell   Ho

n Southern Africa

Mauritius: The Development of a Plural Society

by A.R. Mannick

In the single decade since Mauritius gained its independence, the political and economic development of this densely populated island has been closely watched by all who recognise its strategic location in the Indian Ocean. A member of the OAU and associate member of the EEC, Mauritius has attempted to keep to the path of non-alignment, but recent events such as the leasing of Diego Garcia for use as an American base and the success of a Marxist Party at the 1976 election have put the country at something of a political crossroads.

This book provides a comprehensive picture of Mauritius, its colonial history and present day multi-racial society. Efforts to tackle the problems of unemployment and inequality and government attempts to control its 'sugar barons' and diversify an economy overwhelmingly dependent on sugar production are described in detail.

Cloth £8.50   *Paper £2.95*

African Socialism in Practice
The Tanzanian Experience

edited by Andrew Coulson

What has actually been happening in Tanzania in the twelve years since that country's declaration for 'Socialism and Self-Reliance'? This collection aims to provide an answer, and does so not by presenting a generalised analysis but through a whole series of case studies. The volume reproduces some of the key but lesser known policy documents on Tanzanian socialism as well as President Nyerere's own assessment of 'Ten Years after the Arusha Declaration'.

Fourteen studies, covering rural development and the 'ujamaa' village programme, public enterprise, and education enable readers to judge for themselves to what extent the aspirations formulated by Nyerere have become embodied in practice and the obstacles and difficulties they have encountered.

Cloth £8.95   *Paper £2.95*

ble Street, Nottingham NG7 4ET.